Healing in the Whole Bible

Part One

– Under the Old Testament –

Ken Chant

Healing in the Whole Bible
Part One

– Under the Old Testament –

Ken Chant

Copyright © 2012 Ken Chant
ISBN 978-1-61529-126-7

For information on reordering contact:

Vision Publishing
1672 Main St. E 109
Ramona, CA 92065
1-800-9-VISION
www.booksbyvision.com

A NOTE ON GENDER

It is unfortunate that the English language does not contain an adequate generic pronoun (especially in the singular number) that includes without bias both male and female. So *"he, him, his, man, mankind,"* with their plurals, must do the work for both sexes. Accordingly, wherever it is appropriate to do so in the following pages, please include the feminine gender in the masculine, and vice versa.

FOOTNOTES

A work once fully referenced will thereafter be noted either by "ibid" or "op. cit."

OF MAN'S First Disobedience, and the Fruit
Of that Forbidden Tree, whose mortal taste
Brought Death into the World, and all our woe,
With loss of Eden, till one greater Man
Restore us, and regain the blissful Seat,
Sing Heav'nly Muse, that on the secret top
Of Oreb, or of Sinai, didst inspire
That Shepherd, who first taught the chosen Seed,
In the Beginning how the Heav'ns and Earth
Rose out of Chaos . . . I thence
Invoke thy aid to my adventurous Song,
. . . while it pursues
Things unattempted yet in Prose or Rhyme.
And chiefly Thou O Spirit, that dost prefer
Before all Temples th' upright heart and pure,
Instruct me, for Thou know'st; Thou from the first
Wast present, and with mighty wings outspread
Dove-like satst brooding on the vast Abyss
And mad'st it pregnant: What in me is dark
Illumine, what is low raise and support;
That to the height of this great Argument
I may assert Eternal Providence,
And justify the ways of God to men.

> – John Milton (1608-74)
> *Paradise Lost,* Book One, lines 1-22.

4

CONTENTS

ABBREVIATIONS

Abbreviations commonly used for the books of the Bible are

Genesis	Ge	Habakkuk	Hb
Exodus	Ex	Zephaniah	Zp
Leviticus	Le	Haggai	Hg
Numbers	Nu	Zechariah	Zc
Deuteronomy	De	Malachi	Mal
Joshua	Js		
Judges	Jg		
Ruth	Ru	Matthew	Mt
1 Samuel	1 Sa	Mark	Mk
2 Samuel	2 Sa	Luke	Lu
1 Kings	1 Kg	John	Jn
2 Kings	2 Kg	Acts	Ac
1 Chronicles	1 Ch	Romans	Ro
2 Chronicles	2 Ch	1 Corinthians	1 Co
Ezra	Ezr	2 Corinthians	2 Co
Nehemiah	Ne	Galatians	Ga
Esther	Es	Ephesians	Ep
Job	Jb	Philippians	Ph
Psalm	Ps	Colossians	Cl
Proverbs	Pr	1 Thessalonians	1 Th
Ecclesiastes	Ec	2 Thessalonians	2 Th
Song of Songs	Ca *	1 Timothy	1 Ti
Isaiah	Is	2 Timothy	2 Ti
Jeremiah	Je	Titus	Tit
Lamentations	La	Philemon	Phm
Ezekiel	Ez	Hebrews	He
Daniel	Da	James	Ja
Hosea	Ho	1 Peter	1 Pe
Joel	Jl	2 Peter	2 Pe
Amos	Am	1 John	1 Jn
Obadiah	Ob	2 John	2 Jn
Jonah	Jo	3 John	3 Jn
Micah	Mi	Jude	Ju
Nahum	Na	Revelation	Re

Ca is an abbreviation of *Canticles*, a derivative of the Latin name of the *Song of Solomon*, which is sometimes also called the *Song of Songs*.

PREFACE:

PROSPERITY AND HEALTH

T his is how John expressed his highest wish for the noble Gaius: *"Dear friend, I pray that everything will go well with you and that you will enjoy good health"* (3 Jn 2). Thus he asked for the two boons most people want above all – *prosperity* and *good health*.

But does *God* want us to have these things? When John wanted his friend to enjoy prosperity and good health, was he also giving voice to the will of God?

This study is intended to show that generally speaking [1] it is fair to ask God for health and prosperity, and to expect him to give it. Scripture shows that the ordinary will of God for his people embraces *spiritual*, *mental*, and *physical* soundness (Ac 3:16; 1 Th 5:23).

John understood this when he prayed for Gaius; and there can be little doubt about his confidence that God would grant his request. He was not merely expressing a pious wish; he stated what he wanted for his Christian brother, and he expected to obtain it.

It is my intention to show that the Bible presents to every one of us an offer from God to pardon all our sin and to heal all our sickness. The

---

(1)   That is, within the normal framework of life. Such special exigencies as times of persecution, natural disasters (floods, earthquakes, and the like), or other civic or social disturbances that strike indiscriminately at entire populations, are ordinarily excluded from the promise.

In those instances the healing promise may be worked out in a different form. The same applies to those perils that belong simply to going about the business of living (stumbles, falls, accidents, and losses).

Both scripture and experience show that God intends us to live with risk. Some of the reasons for this state of affairs, and the manner in which such risks may modify the promise, will be discussed later.

plan I have followed is to take the whole Bible, from *Genesis* to *Revelation*, and to show how the scriptures everywhere reveal God's willingness to deliver his people from these twin sorrows: *sin* and *sickness*.

PRELUDE:

BETWEEN TWO STOOLS!

. . . (We) were most interested to hear of the pennyroyal; [2] it is soothing to be reminded that wild nature produces anything ready for the use of man. Men know that *something* is good. One says that it is yellow dock, another that it is bittersweet, another that it is slippery-elm bark, burdock, calamint, elecampane, thoroughwort, or pennyroyal. [3] A man may esteem himself happy when that which is his food is also his medicine. There is no kind of herb but somebody or other says that it is good. I am very glad to hear it. It reminds me of the first chapter of *Genesis*. But how should they know that it is good? That is the mystery to me. I am always agreeably disappointed; it is incredible that they should have found it out. Since all things are good, men fail at last to distinguish which is the bane and which is the antidote. There are sure to be two prescriptions diametrically opposite. Stuff a cold and starve a cold are but two ways. They are the two practices, both always in full blast. Yet you must take advice of the one school as if there was no other.

In respect to religion and the healing art, all nations are still in a state of barbarism. In the most civilised countries the priest is but a Powwow, and the physician a Great Medicine. [4] Consider the deference which is

---

(2) A hairy plant of the mint family, used in herbal medicine.

(3) These are all herbs that were used both as medicines and food in the early 19th-century, particularly in the USA.

(4) That is, the public usually supposes that while priests engage in superstition, physicians deal rather with sober and truly useful remedies.

everywhere paid to a doctor's opinion. Nothing more strikingly betrays the credulity of mankind than medicine. Quackery is a thing universal, and universally successful. In this case it becomes literally true that no imposition is too great for the credulity of men. Priests and physicians should never look one another in the face. [5] They have no common ground, nor is there any to mediate between them. When the one comes, the other goes. They could not come together without laughter, or a significant silence, for the one's profession is a satire on the other's, and either's success would be the other's failure. It is wonderful that the physician should ever die, and that the priest should ever live. Why is it that the priest is never called to consult with the physician? Is it because men believe practically that matter is independent of spirit? But what is quackery? It is commonly an attempt to cure the disease of a man by addressing his body alone. *There is need of a physician who shall minister to both soul and body at once, that is, to man.* Now he falls between two stools. [6]

What Thoreau desired, a "physician who shall minister to both soul and body at once" – that is, to the whole man – has always been here, in the person of Christ the *Great Physician*, whose purpose has always been to bring wholeness to his people, body, soul, and spirit. So then, without falling into quackery, superstition, or even dogmatism, I hope that in these pages [7] you will find an admirable balance between the natural and spiritual worlds, one that will bring medicine and the gospel together in a happy partnership.

---

(5) This sentence, along with the next few, should be read as sarcasm.

(6) Henry David Thoreau (1817-62), American essayist and poet, A Week on the Concord and Merrimack Rivers; The Heritage Press, Norwalk, Connecticut, 1975; pg. 209, 210; emphasis mine.

(7) The same applies to the companion volume to this one, Healing in the Whole Bible – New Testament.

Nonetheless, I am not a physician, and I have no competence in medical science. Which means that this book will necessarily focus on the cure of sickness through the agency of the gospel, yet always with a recognition that God seldom does for us what we can be rightly expected to do for ourselves. He is not prodigal with unnecessary miracles.

> Faith is a fine invention
> For gentlemen who see;
> But microscopes are prudent
> In an emergency! [8]

Or you might prefer Paul's admonition – *"Everything God created is good, and nothing is to be rejected when it is taken with thanksgiving, since it is hallowed by God's own word and by prayer" (1 Ti 4:4, NEB).*

So if you have a headache, take an aspirin! It is a gift of God! Yet do not forget to pray, for in the end there is no healing agent more powerful than a miracle of answered prayer, whether or not it is accompanied by medical intervention!

---

(8)   Emily Dickenson (1830-86); Poems: Second Series (published 1891); "Life #31".

CHAPTER ONE:

IN THE GARDEN OF EDEN

> God sends no sickness into the world but through the
> devil. All sadness and sickness are of the devil, not of
> God. For God permits the devil to harm us because he
> receives little regard from us (Ac 10:38; Lu 13:11).
> Whatever, therefore, pertains to death is the handiwork
> of the devil; and conversely, whatever pertains to life is
> the blessed work of God. . . . The devil must be our Lord
> God's executioner. [9]

L et us begin at the beginning and see how God's desire to keep his
people in good health was accomplished before the *Fall*, and then
before the *Law* –

BEFORE THE FALL

> Now had the Almighty Father from above,
> From the pure Empyrean where he sits
> High Thron'd above all height, bent down his eye,
> His own works and their works at once to view:
> . . . On Earth he first beheld
> Our two first Parents, yet the only two
> Of mankind, in the happy Garden plac'd,
> Reaping immortal fruits of joy and love,
> Uninterrupted joy, unrivall'd love,
> In blissful solitude; . . . ambrosial fragrance fill'd
> All Heav'n, and in the blessed Spirits elect
> Sense of new joy ineffable diffus'd:
> . . . Thus was this place, A happy rural seat of various view:
> Groves whose rich Trees wept odorous Gums and Balm,

(9) Martin Luther (1483-1546); <u>What Luther Says</u>, compiled by Ewald M. Plass;
Concordia Publishing House, St Louis, Missouri.1959; Vol. One, Selection #
1183.

Others whose fruit burnish'd with Golden Rind
Hung amiable, Hesperian Fables true,
If true, here only, and of delicious taste:
Betwixt them Lawns, or level Downs, and Flocks
Grazing the tender herb, were interpos'd,
Or palmy hillock, or the flowery lap
Of some irriguous Valley spread her store,
Flowers of all hue, and without Thorn the Rose:
Another side, umbrageous Grots and Caves
Of cool recess, o'er which the mantling Vine
Lays forth her purple Grape, and gently creeps
Luxuriant; meanwhile murmuring waters fall
Down the slope hills, dispers'd, or in a Lake,
That to the fringed Bank with Myrtle crown'd,
Her crystal mirror holds, unite their streams.
The Birds their choir apply; airs, vernal airs,
Breathing the smell of field and grove, attune
The trembling leaves . . .
Of living Creatures new to sight and strange,
Two of far nobler shape erect and tall,
Godlike erect, with native Honour clad
In naked Majesty seem'd Lords of all,
And worthy seem'd, for in their looks Divine
The image of their glorious Maker shone . . .
So hand in hand they pass'd, the loveliest pair
That ever since in love's embraces met . . .
. . . About them frisking play'd
All Beasts of th' Earth . . .
Sporting the Lion ramp'd, and in his paw
Dandl'd the Kid; Bears, Tigers, Ounces, Pards
Gamboll'd before them, th' unwieldy Elephant
To make them mirth us'd all his might, and wreath'd
His Lithe Proboscis . . . others on the grass
Couch'd, and now fill'd with gazing sat,
Or Bedward ruminating; for the Sun
Declin'd was hasting now with prone career
To th' Ocean Iles, and in th' ascending Scale
Of Heav'n the Stars that usher Evening rose.

— *Paradise Lost*, portions of Books Three & Four.

MADE IN THE LIKENESS OF GOD

See *Genesis 1:26-28,31*. When God made Adam and Eve in his *"image"* he gave them a form that was a reflection of the divine. Built into that first human couple was a resemblance in physical form to the spiritual form of God. Their life came from God, their human personality, the laws of their existence, the nature of their minds, were all based on the divine pattern.

Because of that *"likeness"*, and though they were physical beings, Adam and Eve were able to enjoy free and delightful communion with God. The result of this perfect association was freedom from fear or failure and an unhindered experience of divine blessing and bounty (Ge 2:8-9).

But then they fell into rebellion, and the result was their exclusion from the Garden. They no longer had access to the direct personal presence of God (Ge 3:23-24). However, the basic facts about their creation in the *"image"* and *"likeness"* of God did not change. And we, their children, still possess those same attributes. Though we are marred by sin we bear the form of the divine. [10] Because of this, God is still able to reach out to us, to call to us in the darkness, and we are able to respond.

How do these things relate to sickness and health? In two ways –

- being made in the image of God, the human race was originally created free of any disease; and

- since we still bear the likeness of God, we can be healed of the disease that is now in us.

Let us explore further these two ideas –

---

(10) Should the story of Adam and Eve be read as actual history, or is it poetry conveying divine revelation about the nature of man? For the purpose of this study I am accepting the story as it stands. Various alternative viewpoints are discussed in my book Demonology.

THE DIVINE IMAGE

When God made Adam and Eve in his *"image"* and *"likeness"* he imparted to them the same character as himself. Like God, they were to have a nature of love, truth, holiness, faith, and so on. To enable those various characteristics to function through them, God gave to Adam and Eve three faculties that were outstanding reflections of God: they were given *intelligence, emotion,* and *will.*

By the use of their intelligence, by the expression of emotion, by the authority of their will, they were to reveal the glory of God. The body and the mind God gave them were essentially vehicles to carry those three divine faculties. And crowning all was the human spirit, which gave them access to God and, despite their physical form, transformed them into fundamentally spiritual beings.

THE RESULT OF THE FALL

Sadly, those three faculties, although they are still the mark of divinity in mankind have become desperately corrupted by the Fall –

- human intelligence, which was to have been illuminated and guided by the infinite wisdom of God, became prostituted to the cause of unrighteousness and of ultimate self-destruction.

- human emotion, which was to have been enriched and warmed by the love of God, became explosive with lust and passion.

- human will, which in subjection to the will of God was to have been highly exalted and made the source of universal authority, became an implacable slave-master, driving people into ever deeper subjection to sin and to the judgment of God.

Saddest of all, the human spirit, which was to have been the source of man's friendly and sweet communion with God, became the source of a swelling hubris, a vaunting self-sufficiency, an insufferable conceit, hence also of the total severance of human fellowship with God. From such things stem the sickness that ails our race and the death that destroys us.

Nonetheless, it is plain that man [11] originally abounded with life, and that health, authority, and fellowship with God were his chief joys. All was well, and he prospered. That was God's first desire for the people he had made – and John's prayer shows that it is still his desire. But as John himself suggests, *physical* prosperity and health depend on the prior restoration of *spiritual* life (3 Jn 3b). A man must know that *"all is well with his soul"* before he can pray with confidence for God to heal him physically.

EVERYTHING IN THE GARDEN WAS GOOD

Seven times (itself the biblical number of perfection) we are told that everything God made in the beginning was good. The Hebrew word used here has a wide meaning. Among other lovely things it can be translated *gracious, joyful, pleasant, prosperous, cheerful, bountiful, beautiful, happy, rich*; and so on. Taken together, those expressions convey a picture of life filled with delight and satisfaction, of a world contented and flowing with blessing, of a society righteous and pure, of a universe free of any hurtful thing.

If that picture is applied to the story of creation, then it becomes evident that the world God made was fine in every way. Sin and sickness were foreign to the good earth. They were not there in the beginning. They did not spring from God. And ever since those sorrows first forced themselves upon man, God has sought to deliver his people from them. Observe then, that in the beginning

---

(11) In the next couple of pages (and in other parts of this book) you will find "man", "men", etc, used frequently as generic terms for the human race. If you find this use irritating, please forgive me. I wrote those sentences many years ago, before feminism created a tender conscience about using male terms to include the female. One day I will find the time to re-write them in a more acceptable form. See also the disclaimer on Page 7 above.

MAN HAD DOMINION

> *Then God said . . . let them have dominion . . . over all the earth . . . Be fruitful and multiply, and fill the earth and subdue it; and have dominion over the fish of the sea, and over the birds of the air, and over every living thing that moves upon the earth* (Ge 1:26,28).

What honour and strength were given to man! The whole earth was subject to his command. All that lived was compelled to bow to his will. But note: this was an authority exercised not by physical strength, but through the power of his unsullied faith in God. It was God's good pleasure to dwell with his people, and to make them channels of his own dominion over all material and living things.

Scripture shows that this is still the Lord's wish. Heaven hurts when it sees men and women weakened by sin and crushed by pitiful infirmity. The Father longs to lift his children back to their rightful honour; and over the centuries there have been those who have heeded the divine invitation, and who have seen empires and men, beasts and devils, sin and sickness, fire and water subdued beneath the weight of their faith. I am thinking of Moses, the prophets of Israel, the apostles and disciples of Jesus, *Hebrews 11:32-34*, and, pre-eminently, of Christ himself.

MAN'S GLORIOUS GARMENT

The Bible story leaves an impression that Adam and Eve, before they fell, were clothed in a glorious and beautiful aura. They had no need of material garments, for they were covered by the splendour of God. An illustration of this can be seen in the Lord Jesus Christ, who is spoken of as the *"last Adam"* – that is, in every way he was the archetype of the first Adam. In order to accomplish his mission on earth, Jesus made himself exactly like us. Yet since he was without sin, it seems he had an inherent beauty, a covering of glory, which though usually hidden, he occasionally permitted to radiate (Mt 17:2; Mk 9:2-3; Lu 9:29).

Perhaps Adam and Eve, in their innocent state, were garbed in the same magnificence. Only after they had sinned did they suddenly appear naked to each other, and at once an infinitely poignant longing to recapture at least something of their former beautiful dress possessed them. Their pitiful best was to fabricate a rough garment of leaves; but the Lord in mercy offered on their behalf the first animal sacrifice and permitted them to wear the skins of the beasts.

People driven by lust, or in the black ignorance of a savage state, or in a perversion of decency, have often reduced themselves to nakedness. But when reason and the voice of their own spirits prevail, they recognise that the body is uncomely if publicly deprived of covering (cp. 1 Co 12:23-24). Hence the vast majority of people have sought to clothe themselves – not so much to gain bodily protection as to capture by their garments a lost loveliness and honour. Attractive dress satisfies the cry of the spirit for beauty more than it does the cry of the body for warmth.

Every fashion store displays once again man's original perfection, his fall from grace, his instinctive memory of his former splendour, and his struggle to regain what he has lost. But only the gospel can tell how God has intervened to reveal the inadequacy of all human effort (as he did when he rejected Adam's fig leaves), and how he has made known in Christ his divine method of recovery.

SICKNESS AN INTRUDER

So we are led to believe that sickness was not a part of God's ideal plan – or at least to believe that sickness is fundamentally opposed to God's real desire for his people. When man was made in the likeness of God, when he was clothed in the beauty of the Lord, when he was given great authority, when God said it was all *"very good"*, and when he set our parents among the gay profusion and intoxicating loveliness of Eden, the Lord showed clearly his basic wish. It was that men and women – body, soul, and spirit – should enjoy prosperity, health, and all that can make life good!

There is no reason to suppose God has altered this desire for his children to prosper and be in health. On the contrary –

1) Reason Tells Us

Reason tells us that God, who could create human life in such happiness, can re-create that life, and once again give to men and women freedom from sickness.

If we are sick it is not because God desires it so or takes pleasure in our pain. If we are not healed it is not because God is unable to make us well.

Whatever may be the reason for sickness, whatever may be the cause of our failure to find health, it is not because God is restricted in power or has changed his mind concerning what is *"good"*.

Eden was *"very good"* when sickness was not known: the intrusion of disease did not make it better. This highlights the problem created by those who teach that sickness is a gift from God, sent to enrich our lives. If sickness is *"good"* it is so only in a negative sense – like the pain that warns you to draw your hand out of the fire, like the rod a father brings to his erring son, or like the tolling of a bell that warns of a greater danger threatening. Just as the impersonal savagery of a wild animal reveals a world gone astray, so disease reveals a natural order warped and twisted.

Is it good to be burned? Is it good to be whipped? Is it good to cage an animal? Is it good to be warned of potential disaster? I suppose an affirmative answer can be given; but the goodness in each case is negative; it lacks the positive character of the goodness God saw in his original creation.

Who would imagine the Lord is looking on this present pain-wracked world and still saying, It is *"very good"*? Sin and sickness destroyed the happiness of Eden. Adam and Eve, diseased and dying, were thrust out of the Garden. Sickness was not good; it was the outcropping of evil, the harbinger of death. Surely God hates disease? Surely he is able to heal? Surely he is willing to heal?

But we are not left only to *reason* our way toward an answer, for

2)   *Revelation Tells Us*

Revelation tells us, unequivocally, that God's wish for his people, as far as possible in a world that lies in sin (1 Jn 5:19), is for them to recapture the happiness of Eden.

That is why John prayed for Gaius: *"May all go well for you, and may you be in health"* (3 Jn 2). That is why Paul prayed for his friends, *"May your spirit and soul and body be kept sound and blameless (until) the coming of our Lord Jesus Christ"* (1 Th 5:23). That is why Jesus declared, *"I came that they may have life, and have it more abundantly"* (Jn 10:10).

Do such statements merely express a pious desire, with no real belief that fulfilment is possible? Or do they bear witness that God does indeed want us to prosper and be in health, and that we can pray for this thing with confidence it will be granted?

For my part, I take it that those statements, and others like them, do offer a general promise of abundant life, health, prosperity, and happiness, embracing every part of my being. Nor is the promise for the future only. It is for this present life, valid *"until the coming of our Lord Jesus Christ"*.

So we can say that the Garden of Eden portrays a world created by God without disease; and in doing so reveals

- that sickness is antagonistic to God's original purpose for man;

- that the eradication of sickness must still lie in the will of God;

- that God is able to conquer sickness.

CHAPTER TWO:

THE ORIGIN OF DISEASE

I f God did not create sickness in the beginning, if it was not part of his original design for the human race, then how did it originate? If sickness was an intruder into the Garden of Eden, if it is foreign to real life and happiness and opposed to what is truly good, then why doesn't the Lord simply remove it?

BORN TO DIE

SICKNESS DEFINED

It has been said that we begin to die as soon as we are born, and that every occurrence of disease is an outcropping of this inexorable law of death. Sickness is the shadow of the grave. Our diseases are the harbinger of our death. In one way or another all disease is incipient death; and even if, like Lazarus and Hezekiah (Jn 11:4; Is 38:1), a person is reprieved from the jaws of darkness, the delay is only temporary. People do not die because they become sick, they become sick because they are dying.

If then we can discover the cause of death, we shall have found the origin of sickness. And this holds true even in the case of people who seemingly never suffer from illness: even for them, when the wizened stalk of life is finally cut by the Reaper's scythe, it falls only because the tough fibre has been continually weakened by the inward ravages of disease. The forces of life, finally exhausted, collapse before the stronger forces of destruction.

THE ORIGIN OF DEATH

The question *"whence cometh death?"* is easily answered, for scripture plainly declares what has brought the sentence of death so heavily upon mankind – *sin* (Ge 2:17; Ro 5:12; 6:23). The declaration stands solemn and immutable: *"The soul that sins shall die"*(Ez 18:4,20). Because we sin, we are sick; because we are sick, we die. More will be said about that later, but for now let us trace back further: where did sin originate?

Again the answer is clear: *"Through one man sin came into the world and death through sin"* (Ro 5:12). That man, of course, was Adam, with his wife Eve.

But there is still one more question to ask before the whole problem is solved, and that is, what agent caused Adam and Eve to sin? Again the answer is plain: sin found its beginning in the subtlety of the serpent, that is, the devil, or Satan (Ge 3:1, ff.) [12] Satan is the cause of sin; it was he who brought down upon himself and upon the men and woman the curse of God's broken law; it is he who holds the power of death over humanity (He 2:14). And that curse, as far as the human race is concerned, has brought multiplied pain (Ge 3:16-19). How fearful the abyss of suffering and sickness implied in those words!

So we can conclude:

1) all sickness stems indirectly from Satan – scripture says, for example, that all the thousands of people whom Jesus healed were "oppressed by the devil" (Ac 10:38).

2) some sickness is directly caused by Satan – as, for example, when the devil struck down Job (2:7).

3) all sickness arises indirectly from sin – that is, because the human race is corrupted by sin, it is also stricken by the indiscriminate ravages of sickness.

For example, we are told that the results of parents' sins may fasten onto their children to the third and fourth generation (Ex 20:5; 34:7; Nu 14:18; De 5:9).

4) some sickness is caused directly by sin.

For example, Jesus warned a man, *"Sin no more, or something worse may befall you"* (Jn 5:14), thus implying that his sickness had arisen from his sin, and that further sin could bring on him a more grievous affliction.

---

(12) Angelology and Demonology (the study of the doctrine of angels and of the devil) are examined in my books of the same names.

Sickness, then, is attributable to God only insofar as it is the penalty laid down for violation of his righteous law, or only insofar as our fallen state compels God to use disease as a method of discipline or of drawing us to maturity. But the true and direct cause of human suffering is centred in sin and the oppression of Satan. As long as the devil and iniquity hold sway in human affairs so long will sickness have access to us and power over us. [13]

BEFORE THE LAW

From Adam until today people everywhere have feared and hated sickness, and have striven to banish it from their lives. Our entire society continually views disease as an enemy and exerts itself mightily toward the goal of either eliminating sickness, or at least of minimising its effect on those who are ill.

Even those who encourage people to be patient in their afflictions, and to accept illness as God's will, nonetheless urge the sufferers to use every possible medical aid to ease their pain and to hasten their recovery. Yet it would seem more logical to assert that only those who believe that God is opposed to sickness are really free to seek medical aid! Those who believe their illness is God's will should surely make no effort toward recovery, but should simply resign themselves to heaven's mysterious purpose!

But despite the sophistries of some religious teachers, sick people in every generation have instinctively resorted to prayer, sensing that illness is their enemy, hoping that divine power might restore them to health.

So it was in the centuries between Adam and Moses. Nowhere can you find people accepting disease as a blessing to be received with thanksgiving. Rather, they recognised the evil of illness and earnestly sought healing from the Lord God.

---

(13) The advances of medical science cannot alter this principle, for doctors deal only with the surface aspect of disease, they cannot touch the deeper working of sickness, that law of inner decay, which draws us irresistibly to death.

However, not having a definite covenant of healing, nor any unequivocal promise on which to build their faith, they were able to pray only in *hope* that God might grant their desire. Being unsure of God's will they were not able to do any more than commit themselves to the mercy of God.

Nonetheless, though the time had not yet come for God to enter into a definite contract of healing with his people, those who had close fellowship with him still knew intuitively that the Lord was opposed to disease and death. This inner certainty drove them to plead with God to deliver those who were tormented and bound. And from time to time the Lord showed his desire and his power to heal by the miracles he wrought.

By contrast, there were other occasions when God, in punishment for sin, inflicted sickness upon various individuals, and even upon whole groups of people. The following references illustrate these things. But before looking at them let us confront an objection.

Some people are offended by the idea of God himself "inflicting disease", and would prefer to say something like, "he **_allows_** disease to be inflicted." They are adamant that God is never the *immediate* cause of sickness, that he never uses sickness as the direct agent of his judgment, that his hand never imposes affliction upon any of his children, that infirmity may be caused by Satan, sin, or nature, but never by God. I am sympathetic with this, but must stick to the above wording, simply because it happens to be biblical (as many references in these pages will show). It may suit some piece of dogma to deny that God himself ever makes anyone sick, but it hardly matches numerous plain biblical statements. The Bible should shape our theology, not the reverse!

Others argue that while sickness may be a *penalty* of sin, God himself does not *impose* it. Yet that is like saying that a criminal is in jail by his own choice, penalised in reality by his own hand rather than by the judge. But that is surely just a play on words. In real life we neither think nor speak like that, and nor does the Bible. Certainly, if the prisoner had not broken the law he would not be in prison; nonetheless, it was the judge who put him there. Likewise, God has decreed that disease will be one of the penalties for violating his commands, and who can take away from him the right to execute that penalty whenever he may justly do so? To say that he uses the devil as the agent of his judgment no more absolves God from responsibility for his righteous sentence than a judge can abrogate his responsibility by saying that it was a policeman who actually incarcerated the wrongdoer.

Admittedly, an entirely logical and formally consistent theology yearns to prove that God is never the direct cause of disease. But the Bible declines to sit in our boxes. In theory, it would be nice to say that God merely allows sickness, but never inflicts it; but neither scripture nor life allows such tidy doctrines or careful terminology. The Bible is more human and relaxed than our neat formulations desire it to be!

SICKNESS AND DELIBERATE SIN

The Bible leaves no doubt that sickness is sometimes linked directly to sin.

The Sodomites were stricken with blindness by the angel of the Lord (Ge 19:11 – although the nature of this "blindness" may have been psychological rather than physical). Shortly afterward, because of total refusal by the people to repent, the whole city was destroyed (vs. 24-25). Whatever the true nature of the "blindness", and of the destruction that overthrew Sodom and Gomorrah, this story establishes an early link between disease, natural disaster, and the judgment of God.

SICKNESS AND UNKNOWN SIN

See *Genesis 12:17-20; 20:1-18*. These two stories tell how God struck Pharaoh and Abimelech, and their households, and laid them under sentence of death, because of their crime against Abraham. However, because they had acted in ignorance, Pharaoh and Abimelech were given an opportunity to repent, to rectify their fault, and to be healed.

Note especially that healing did not come to Abimelech (nor possibly to Pharaoh also) until Abraham prayed for him. Abimelech had no covenant relationship with God, there was no certain basis upon which he could pray, nor upon which God could answer his prayer. But Abraham was a *"prophet"* (20:7), and God promised Abimelech that if he heeded the Lord's command and requested Abraham's prayers, he would be healed. Abimelech complied with God's demands, *"and Abraham prayed to God; and God healed Abimelech, and also healed his wife and female slaves . . . "* (vs. 17).

Observe that in these first three stories from Genesis (the earliest records we have) sickness is closely linked with sin. Then to this is added the further arresting fact that the first incident of healing on record took place in response to prayer. It is frequently true that the first mention in scripture of a subject establishes its basic meaning throughout the remainder of the Bible; and this appears to be the case here. So those two accounts establish what is confirmed in almost every other part of scripture, namely, *the connection between sin and sickness, prayer and healing.*

Of course, those stories do not teach that all sin results in sickness, nor that all sickness arises from sin. God has various methods of dealing with sin, and sickness may be caused by factors quite divorced from sin. But the stories do establish at least some causal relationship between sin and sickness, and they definitely set a precedent of prayer to God for healing.

THREE RIGHTEOUS WOMEN

We come now to Sarah, Rebecca, and Rachel, who, either through illness or congenital malfunction, were not able to bear children (Ge 21:5-7; 25:20-21; 30:22-24). The three women all thought of their infirmity as something evil, a reproach to them, and they fervently desired God to grant them a miracle of healing. They were given their request.

But once again, since there was as yet no specific promise of healing for the women to claim, they could pray only in hope that God would show them mercy. But it was a hope that pleased God, and he honoured their expectation with a miracle.

THE SIGN GIVEN TO MOSES

Moses was told to *"put his hand into his bosom . . . and when he took it out, behold, his hand was leprous, as white as snow . . . and he put his hand into his bosom again; and when he took it out, behold, it was restored like the rest of his flesh" (Ex 4:6-7).*

That arresting sign was given to Moses and Israel to demonstrate the sovereign power of God both to inflict disease, and to heal it. Just as cancer is hated and feared in our day, so was leprosy in the ancient world. The Lord gave Moses this startling leprous sign, first, to show the Egyptians how easily God could cause the entire empire of the Nile to decay and die, and second, to show Israel that their God was able to deliver them from even the most dreadful scourge.

SUMMARY AND CONCLUSION

We conclude that in patriarchal times no-one ever accepted sickness as a blessing to be desired; it was always thought of as a curse, a captivity, something evil, foreign to God's ordinary will for his people. However, it was also recognised that God was sovereign, that nothing could take place outside his will, and it was generally believed that disease and suffering were divine judgments that followed in the wake of spiritual failure.

Faced with such beliefs, being uncertain of God's promise, not having a specific covenant of healing upon which to base a positive claim for deliverance, they could only pray and throw themselves onto the mercy of the Lord. But many did pray with such earnestness and deep desire that heaven heard their cry and made them whole. Yet untold thousands more simply resigned themselves to disaster and did whatever they could to comfort themselves.

Today, among people who do not know the covenant of healing that God has established, the same position obtains. A few, by dint of fervent pleading, may succeed in gaining a miracle of answered prayer; but the great majority either ignore God in their sickness or passively accept it as God's will. They do indeed exert prodigious effort to get well by medical means, but they have no confidence in the power of God to heal.

CHAPTER THREE:

HEALING UNDER THE LAW

I t is a remarkable indictment against the church today that so many people are completely unaware the Lord God made a definite covenant of healing with Israel. This promise of divine healing was incorporated into the laws of Moses, and it was intended to draw Israel to trust in God as the nation's Great Physician. I want to consider the promise itself first of all, then, in subsequent chapters, the foundations upon which the promise was to be fulfilled, and then examples of its fulfilment.

THE COVENANT OF HEALING

AN UNEQUIVOCAL PROMISE

EXODUS 15:26

Nothing could be plainer than the words, *"I will put none of (these) diseases upon you . . . for I am the Lord, your healer."* Here is an unequivocal promise of a cure for sickness. More, it is a promise, not merely of healing, but also of protection from and prevention of disease. It was given to the whole nation: no limit of person, time, or place was put upon it. It was a promise that enabled any person in Israel to call upon the Lord and to be cured of any disease. [14]

EXODUS 23:25-26

Again the Lord made a plain promise to remove sickness out of the land, and to bless the people with health and joy, in their eating and drinking,

---

(14) I am not forgetting that the healing promise, here and everywhere in scripture, is linked with a demand for obedience and faith; but those aspects of our relationship to the healing covenant will be discussed later.

their working and playing, on the land and in their homes. This promise has both a natural and a supernatural outworking –

1) *Natural*

Behind the promise lies the simple fact that obedience to the laws of God is automatically conducive to good health.

The laws God gave Israel established (for those days) remarkable standards of hygiene and good diet. They preserved the integrity of the family and they gave security to the young, the aged, the weak, and the defenceless. They relieved anxiety and stress, they provided for a full day of rest every seventh day, they brought relief from guilt, and they protected property rights.

Inevitably, if Israel had observed those laws, sickness in the land would have been minimised. Insofar as the laws of Moses are generally observed in our land today, we have gained the benefit of a comparatively healthy population. [15]

2) *Supernatural*

Beyond this natural and more or less spontaneous outworking of good health, the promise of healing also contains a supernatural element. Nationally, whenever plague, drought, or any form of disaster struck Israel, the promises provided a basis upon which the people could cry out to God for deliverance. And, as we shall see, many times God honoured such a cry. Personally, whenever an individual citizen became ill, he could call upon the Lord and be made whole – and again the scripture contains many examples of personal miracles of healing.

Between those two elements of the promise there was continual interplay. The good health of the individual depended largely on belonging to a healthy community, which in turn depended on how closely the

---

(15) That is, the general principles, the basic concepts, that underlie the laws of Moses are almost all built into our modern statutes and practices. Compare with this the fearfully high incidence of disease found, say, in many eastern nations whose laws and customs do not reflect the wisdom of the Mosaic precepts.

community adhered to the divine statutes. The supernatural aspect of the promise did not permit wilful violation of its natural aspect. Nonetheless, if sickness arose, whether from violation of God's law, or from some other cause, the nation or the individual could always flee to God in hope of a miracle. The same is true today.

LEVITICUS 26:3-13

What a stirring enumeration of the immense benefits and blessings the Lord was willing to heap upon Israel in their individual, social, spiritual, commercial, corporate and national life! There was no limit to the health, happiness, and prosperity God was willing to give them.

But the promise was dependent upon the nation walking in his statutes and keeping his commandments. If they broke his laws and violated his ordinances God warned that misery and desolation would overtake them (vs. 14-39).

Notice how this judgment, just like the covenant of healing, also has a natural and a supernatural aspect –

- *natural*, because the broken law automatically produced a crop of ailments and afflictions; and

- *supernatural*, because the Lord God was able to (and frequently did) intervene personally to inflict his fury upon a sinning people.

However, the threat of disaster was followed immediately by a consoling promise: if the people chose to repent and confess their wrong-doing, then God undertook to remember his covenant with them and to restore them again to all their lost privileges and blessings (vs. 40-46).

DEUTERONOMY 7:13-15; 28:1-14

How staggering are those promises in their abundance and richness! Every aspect of life is covered. Every good thing is included. No desirable blessing is omitted. Everything the people could possibly want or need, and much more beside, is offered to them – along with a strong assurance that all sickness and every enemy would be banished from the land. Can it be denied that passages such as those show God's chief desire for his people is to bring them into the highest possible fullness and satisfaction in this life?

The old Puritan catechism asked: "What is God's chief end in creating man?" And the expected answer was: "The happiness of man." How true! God made us to be happy! And in this present life, full happiness is inextricably bound up with physical well-being.

Some rejoin that it is better to be physically ill and spiritually well than to be spiritually ill and physically well. Of course – if we have to make such a choice. But that false dichotomy is not found in scripture. The Bible does not view man as a spirit dwelling in a body that brings him more nuisance than benefit; rather, it views man as a composite whole, requiring both body and spirit to be truly human. The biblical ideal is that spiritual and physical health should go hand in hand. Perish the thought that God wants us to be miserable here so that we can be merry in heaven!

There are two strong expressions in the passage just cited (7:15) –

1)   *"All Sickness"*

The Hebrew word is *choli*, and it definitely refers to physical illness (see De 28:59; 1 Kg 17:17; 2 Kg 13:14; Is 38:9; etc.) In each instance *choli* is translated "sickness" or "illness". The same word is also rendered "disease" or "grief" (see 2 Ch 16:12; 21:18; Is 53:3-4). Its meaning is plain: God desires to take away from us all disease and illness; he wants to remove from us the pain and grief of sickness; he wants us to have health and prosperity.

2)   *"Evil Diseases"*

The word for "disease" is *madveh*, which means simply "sickness". It is translated as "disease" here and in *28:60*. "Evil" is the Hebrew word *ra*, which occurs scores of times in scripture, especially in connection with sin and the works of Satan. It means literally, "bad".

So the Bible does not pretend that sickness and disease are good: they are bad. They come from the evil heart of Satan; they arise from human sin. Even if God makes use of disease to chastise, discipline, or judge, it still remains his general will that we be wholly delivered from sickness.

Certainly there were conditions attached to the promise, and there were many things that prevented Israel from realising the wonderful potential of what God offered. But this does not alter the fact that the promise revealed God's real desire for those who loved him and served him truly.

Notice again that while scripture obliges me to acknowledge that God may and does use sickness as a means of punishment or of discipline, always the intent of the Bible is to show that the Father yearns for his people to repent, to rise up in faith, and to be made whole. True, those who violate God's law will eventually have to accept the consequences, which sometimes include illness; but equally truly, those who turn to the Lord and trust his promise are assured of his mercy and may firmly hope for a miracle!

DEUTERONOMY 28:15-68

Notice especially vs. 15-24, 27-29, 35, 58-61.

In that dreadful recital of curses against a sinning people, plague, pestilence, and disease occupied a prominent place. Such a bitter association of sickness with the broken law of God – with sin – strongly isolates disease and identifies it as a curse upon humanity. It is not a mark of divine pleasure, but of displeasure. In fact, everywhere in scripture, good health is associated with the blessing and favour of God, while disease is associated either with the broken law, divine discipline, or divine judgment. [16]

DEUTERONOMY 30:15-20

The choice is plain, the promise is clear. Life, health, abundant blessing, and all good things are promised to the people – not in the world to come, but in their own world – if they will only *"love the Lord their God and obey his voice"*. But if they failed to heed his voice and transgressed his law, then cursing and evil would become their unhappy lot.

---

(16) This is not to say that every time a person gets sick he or she is being judged by God or is out of favour with God, nor am I saying that good health by itself is a mark of divine favour. Far from it! The position with regard to individual cases will be clarified as this study proceeds. I am stating only what is true of the community as a whole, and generally true of us as individuals. God's favour issues in good health, while sickness may be a mark of divine displeasure, or at least, of the fact that God's laws have been broken in some way.

INTERPRETING THE COVENANT

The above references seem to provide compelling evidence that, among many other things, the Lord God specifically committed himself to be the Healer of Israel. He required only that they believe his precepts. On that condition he undertook not only to heal them whenever they became ill, but even further, actually to rid their community of disease.

If that were not what the promise meant, then the words of God would seem to be shockingly untrustworthy. If the Bible is truly the inspired word of God, then the promise can hardly mean anything less than this: God is designating himself the Great Physician of his people. He swore to be their Healer and their Health, their Physician and their Protector. Nor can the promise be made to apply only to the world to come; it refers in the plainest possible terms to the daily life of the people in their own land.

THREE DIFFERENT APPROACHES

There are three possible reactions to this covenant of divine healing –

1) The promises can be rejected as preposterous; the biblical record can be discounted as unreliable; the accounts of the promise and the stories of its fulfilment can be read as religious fables – in other words, God never did make a covenant of healing with Israel.

Many modern commentators, who then deny any probability of divine healing being available in answer to prayer, **adopt that stance. They generally look on sickness as simply a natural fact**or in human life, in which God involves himself mainly by giving man skill in the practice of medicine, and by giving sufferers the strength patiently to bear their afflictions.

Obviously that is not an interpretation I can accept. [17]

---

(17) It is, of course, correct to say that all medical knowledge ultimately stems from God, and that God does convey divine strength to all who seek his help in suffering. I am only affirming that God's involvement in the problem of sickness does not end there.

(1) The promises can be accepted as reliable, and it can be acknowledged that the Lord did make a clear healing covenant with Israel. But, it is said, the covenant has now been abrogated, and it no longer lies in the purpose of God to maintain a promise of healing for his people.

One of the commentators on my shelf puts it this way: "Prosperity was the blessing of God under the old dispensation, but under the new his blessing is found in adversity." The same writer goes on to say that God showed his favour toward his people of old by giving them wealth, but he shows his favour toward his people today by denying them prosperity and by taking them through the dark valley of pain. Suffering, he says, is the hallmark of God's special favour today, the highest gift of his love!

Now if that author had meant there are occasions when it is kinder of God to hurt than to heal, to inflict pain than to give prosperity, it would be impossible to disagree with him – scripture itself abundantly teaches that lesson. But if he means (as he does) that the covenant of healing has been cancelled, and not only cancelled but so radically changed that the Father now finds more delight in the tears of his children than he does in their laughter, then scripture pours scorn on his ideas. And so do I.

(2) The promises can be accepted as a simple revelation of God's basic desire for his people of every generation. And though the outward provisions of the covenant may have become substantially different, its inner promise of health and prosperity is established today on a foundation even stronger than that given to Israel. And that, of course, is the view followed in these notes.

THE PLACE OF ADVERSITY

A distinction must be made between the general promise of God to his people as a whole, and the particular circumstances that may surround the life of an individual person. Generally, as we have seen and shall continue to see, the Lord desires health and prosperity for his people, and you and I may usually turn that general promise into a particular one, applicable to our own lives. However, it must also be recognised that adversity and affliction have a definite place in the economy of God.

That aspect of divine providence will be considered in detail when we study the story of Job; but at this point I want to show you briefly how adversity and affliction are used by God –

1) against sinners, by way of judgment for sin. Various examples will be discussed as we come to them. It should be noted that in such cases the afflicted person is usually free to repent, and to claim both the Lord's pardon and the Lord's healing.

2) on behalf of the godly, by way of fatherly discipline and chastisement, for the purpose of better perfecting in their lives the character of the Lord and his divine will (cp. He 12:6-11).

3) on behalf of the godly in the form of persecution for righteousness' sake – and at such times the people of God gladly suffer all manner of insult and hurt, if only the honour of their Saviour may be increased (cp. Ac 5:41; 9:16; Ro 8:17; 2 Co 1:6-7; 11:23-27; 2 Ti 2:12; Mt 5:11; 10:22).

In the two latter cases I am unable to deny that affliction will ever take the form of sickness, for the story of Job shows otherwise. But it may be said that where sickness does occur as a result of fatherly discipline, the true *"end of the Lord"* (as in the case of Job, Ja 5:11) will normally be found in healing, not in permanent paralysis or death.

Where sickness occurs as a result of persecution then it may indeed be unto death and part of the cross we are called to bear for Christ. But such instances are surely rare, and removed from the ordinary providence of God. For the great majority of people the will of God lies in his promise of health and prosperity. It is noteworthy that John offered his prayer for the health and prosperity of his friend Gaius, at a time when persecution of the church was widespread (3 Jn 2). Many Christians were being cruelly put to death; but for those whose lives were spared the general promise was still valid: that they might be healthy and happy. [18]

_____

(18) We observe here the tension that does exist between the general promise of healing and the specific providence of God. This apparent contradiction is the source of the anguish found in many of the *Psalms*; and it is especially exemplified in *Job*. However, this tension exists throughout scripture, and the Christian must learn to relate to it by faith. Our study of *Job* will offer some guidelines for that faith.

FOUR SUPPORTING ARGUMENTS

These studies will show that the healing covenant God made with Israel has in fact been enlarged, restructured, and reinforced by a new covenant made with the Church. But even if it could be shown that the original covenant has been annulled and not replaced by another, we could still indirectly conclude that God desires healing and health for his people. That conclusion could be based on ideas like the following –

1) God is not a respecter of persons. As the song-writer declared, "What he has done for others, he will do for you!" If God, in history, has healed thousands of people in response to their repentance and faith, then we believe he is willing to heal all who are sick. Is not his pardon of even one person's sin accepted as a demonstration of his willingness to forgive all who come to him with faith? Surely the same argument is applicable to healing?

2) God is the same today as he was yesterday, he changes not (cp. Ps 33:11; 102:27; Ma 3:6; He 13:8). If the pain-filled cry of a sick person has moved his compassion in the past, will it not still do so? If faith tapped his healing power in the past, will it not still do so? Has his compassion changed? Have his values altered? Does faith no longer reach him? Has he now become the Great Afflicter and no longer the Great Physician?

3) God has given us today a better promise and a better covenant than was given to Israel of old (cp. He 7:19,22; 8:6; 9:23; 10:34; 11:16,35). I cannot believe that God has made the new covenant better than the old by offering sickness instead of health, poverty in place of prosperity, misery in place of merriment, sighing instead of singing, and so on.

I admit that within the Christian context it is sometimes possible to give the word "better" a higher "spiritual" sense. In other words, it can be said to refer to the better grace, the richer joy, the deeper satisfaction God gives to those who endure suffering for Christ's sake. And it is true that those high blessings are more freely available to us than they were to Israel of old. It is also true that the gospel of Christ does introduce us to a deeper spiritual experience, a more mature insight, a greater comprehension of eternal reality than the saints of old knew. And there is indeed a wonderful grace of God available to those who must endure privation and pain for the sake of the gospel.

But while full allowance may be made for that special, and rather subtle, Christian use of the word "better", it must also be recognised that the times when Christians are thrust into the fiery furnace of affliction are comparatively rare. In normal times "better" must surely carry its normal meaning.

Essentially, there was only one ordinary and natural way in which the old covenant could have been bettered, and that was to make its promises more comprehensive, and to make easier the terms on which those promises could be appropriated. In fact, that is just what Christ has done.

So the promise is now no longer restricted to Israel, but is extended to the entire world. It now embraces heaven and earth, including a future inheritance as well as present prosperity. It now has a much stronger foundation (laid in Christ, rather than in the mute beasts of Moses); and the terms of the covenant have been reduced to the simplest possible formula: *"believe in the Lord Jesus Christ and you will be healed!"*

4)   Scripture says we should think of God as our Father and ourselves as his children. But that comparison has no meaning if it does not mean that our relationship with God contains the qualities ordinarily seen in the relationship between a father and his children. Which means

- what we expect our children to be to us, so must we be to God: loving, obedient, giving him honour, and showing implicit trust in his word. But also the reverse:

- God thinks of us as we do our own children, and has the same desires for his children as we do.

What do you desire for your children – that they should be poor, diseased, defeated, broken? Hardly! God himself expects all parents to work for, pray for, the health, happiness, and prosperity of their children. His attitude as a Father toward us, his children, is the same (cp. Mt 6:25-34; 7:7-11). Our pleasure is his delight; our pain is his grief.

Certainly, like any father, if we are disobedient children he must chastise us (He 12:5-11). Further, the process of education, of training from spiritual infancy to maturity, is not always pleasant. It may sometimes involve hardship and suffering. Like the psalmist, we may sometimes have to pass through the valley of the shadow of death – but only to come out of the valley refined, able to sit at the table of the Lord, anointed with the oil of joy, drinking the cup of gladness, and experiencing the goodness and mercy of the Lord all the days of our lives!

CHAPTER FOUR:

THE EXODUS AND BEYOND

T he previous chapters have established some of the general reasons why we believe God has established a healing covenant with his people. We are glad to call him our Great Physician. And that same refrain was sung from the days of Adam until Moses. But was it still sung after the law was given to Israel? Did the statutes of Moses change the practice of divine healing in Israel?

There were indeed some changes, as we shall see. But the covenant of healing itself remained powerful and effective under the direction of Moses –

EXODUS 4:6-7

The sign of Moses' leprous hand was an eloquent demonstration of God's ability to afflict sorely the impenitent, and to heal those who called upon him for deliverance.

EXODUS 4:24-26

This obscure incident is as baffling to modern commentators as it was to ancient Jewish scholars; but the basic lesson is clear: Moses was stricken with sickness, in fact threatened with death, because of his failure to circumcise his son. The curse was averted only when Zipporah fulfilled the requirements of the covenant.

Circumcision was "a symbol of putting away all that was unpleasing to God"; it signified a total commitment to the covenant; in its hygienic aspect it typified the healing promise. By assenting to Zipporah's act in circumcising their son, Moses reinforced his obedience and faith, and the divine response was immediate: *"the Lord let him alone."*

THE PLAGUES ON EGYPT

Namely: of Blood (Ex 7:19-21); of Frogs (8:5-6); of Lice (8:16-17); of Flies (8:20-24); upon the Cattle (9:1-7); of Boils (9:8-11); of Hail (9:22-

26); of Locusts (10:12-15); of Darkness (10:21-23); of the Angel of Death (12:29-30).

During all of those plagues, though appalling devastation and suffering fell upon Egypt, the land of Goshen (where the Israelites lived) was kept free. This, God said, was a powerful sign of his awesome might both to destroy and to deliver.

That divine ability has not changed, and neither has the heart of God toward his people. There is a "Goshen" for all who believe today, a place of refuge, of salvation and healing: it is found in the Lord Jesus Christ.

EXODUS 32:35; NUMBERS 11:33-35

A plague slew many of the people because of their sin against God in the matter of the golden calf, and their lusting after the flesh of the quails: thus confirming that even the people of the covenant can fall beneath God's blow if they yield to intemperance and passion.

A question may arise here (also in connection with the other miracles surrounding the story of the exodus) about how much natural factors were involved in these accounts of plague and curse – that is, factors such as inadequate housing, improper diet, crowded conditions, desert environment, and so on?

Almost certainly such natural factors do underlie many of the accounts, if not all of them (cp. the wind that drove back the Red Sea, Ex 14:21). But two other things must also be said:

1) The stance of the Bible (especially the OT) is that nothing can happen outside the will of God; behind every event the hand of God is recognised.

One of the remarkable characteristics of the ancient Hebrews was their refusal to see anything apart from God – every event in their lives, and in the world around them, was interpreted within their belief that God was continually and actively involved in the world he had created. The natural and the supernatural were continually fused together in their minds; they refused to contemplate any event as happening without God. [19]

This attitude disposed them to call some events miracles or acts of God that we might prefer to describe as merely natural or providential happenings. Yet we are the losers by our failure to be deeply conscious of the presence of God and to perceive the working of God in the daily events of life. To the Hebrew, nothing was a coincidence; the timing and ordering of all events were witnesses to God's care of his people. Whether or not God chose to use natural means, the user was still GOD, and that, for the Hebrew, transformed the event into a miracle!

2) However, even though some of the biblical "miracles" may be wholly susceptible to a natural explanation, many others surpass all ordinary explanation, whether in their very nature or in the exceptional results achieved. For example: natural explanations may be suggested for some of the plagues that devastated Egypt (although there was certainly a miracle in their precise timing), but how can the slaying of the first-born (only) of man and beast be explained apart from a direct act of God? A strong wind may have parted the Red Sea, but what about the extraordinary (supernatural?) pillar of cloud by day and of fire by night that guided Israel through the wilderness?

> When Israel, of the Lord beloved,
>   Out from the land of bondage came,
> Her fathers' God before her moved,
>   An awful Guide in smoke and flame.
> By day, along the astonished lands

---

(19) A graphic example of this principle can be seen in *Psalm 29*, which is actually a description of a thunderstorm. We tend to think of a storm as a purely natural phenomenon, and we are able to offer a scientific explanation for each of its characteristics. The psalmist was just as aware as we are of this natural aspect; but he was even more vividly aware of the invisible presence of God behind the storm. This overwhelming mindfulness of God enabled him to write one of the most magnificent descriptions of a thunderstorm in all literature. He observed, inextricably involved with the natural phenomena of the storm, the supernatural presence and power of the Lord God.

> The cloudy pillar glided slow;
> By night, Arabia's crimsoned sands
>   Returned the fiery column's glow.
>
> But present still, though now unseen!
>   When brightly shines the prosperous day,
> Be thoughts of Thee a cloudy screen
>   To temper the deceitful ray.
> And oh, when stoops on Judah's path
>   In shade and storm the frequent night,
> Be Thou, long-suffering, slow to wrath,
>   A burning and a shining light! (20)

NUMBERS 12:10-16

Miriam was severely stricken with leprosy, and then healed again. She was afflicted because she had lifted herself up in pride and had criticised Moses (vs. 1-2); she was healed when Aaron spoke on her behalf, expressing her sorrow and repentance, and when Moses prayed for her (vs. 11-13).

Notice the boldness and authority, the faith, of Moses' prayer: *"Heal her NOW, O God!"* But also his humility: *"I beseech thee!"* Even so, it was seven days before she was fully recovered and permitted to move amongst the people again.

There seems to be no reason why the same scenario may not be often repeated. Pride and rebellion against God may be a cause of sickness; but repentance, coupled with the prayer of faith, can still bring a miracle of healing. And God, for the purpose of discipline and to induce a chastened attitude, may still test faith by delaying full recovery.

NUMBERS 16:31-35, 41-50

The sudden death of the rebellious prince Korah and his followers was followed by a plague that killed nearly fifteen thousand of the people.

---

(20) From *Rebecca's Song*, in <u>Ivanhoe</u>, by Sir Walter Scott.

The whole nation was threatened with destruction, until Aaron hurriedly took steps to make atonement and to stay the course of the pestilence. What was the nature of the plague? What were its natural causes? We do not know. Moses simply makes the stark declaration: *"Wrath has gone forth from the Lord; the plague has begun!"*

Does God then send sickness?

Some claim that God is the author of sickness only in a permissive sense, that he never directly inflicts a disease upon anyone. The question is a nice one. But Moses would plainly answer that whether the plague arose from natural causes, or only from the permissive will of God, it still came from God. God was actively, not passively, involved in its coming. It was an expression of heaven's wrath, and had to be met by offering atonement within the terms of the covenant.

So Aaron hastened to stand between the dead and the living, to make atonement for the people, and the plague was stopped.

The story teaches us that

- sickness may strike the disobedient as a mark of divine displeasure, and that

- prompt appropriation of God's provision of atonement and healing can provide an effective cure, and that

- there are times when death may strike too quickly to leave room for repentance (for the 15,000 no remedy was left).

We need the fear of God, as well as faith in him!

So this account gives a graphic illustration of offended divine justice compelled to punish wrongdoers; yet at the same time divine mercy reaches out with a method of healing. This has always been, and still is, God's way. Though he must show wrath, he will also show kindness; he always provides a way of escape for those who are willing to seek it. Behold the severity of God; but also his goodness! To those who fall he must be severe; but to those who turn back to him he will show good! (Ro 11:22).

NUMBERS 25:1-9

Occasioned by the harlotry of Israel with the Midianites, a plague broke out that killed 24,000 people. The lesson here is much the same as before, but with this difference: the plague was not stayed until the people took definite action to remove the cause of their troubles. They stood weeping before the Lord, but God did not heed them until forcible steps had been taken to remove the open sin.

Many people since then have had their prayers unanswered because of the same failure. It is not enough merely to lament suffering, nor even to be sorry for sin; the transgression that is often the cause of our hurt must be sternly removed. The scripture says: *"If I cherish iniquity in my heart, the Lord will not listen"* (Ps 66:18). Put to death that darling sin, and then you will be able to quote the next verse: *"But God has listened; he has given heed to the voice of my prayer"*. Blessed be God!

PSALM 105:37

> *He led forth Israel with silver and gold, and there were none among his tribes who stumbled. Other translations read: There were no sick and feeble folk among them then . . . There were no invalids among his tribes . . . Among all their tribes no man fell . . . There were none among the people who faltered through disease . . . Among their tribes there was not one who was lame or halt.*

It is impossible to say how literally we should take those statements. Perhaps they are merely poetic hyperbole, conveying only a colourful picture of vigorously healthy tribes, ready for marching and war. There may in fact have been some lame, diseased, and feeble people among them.

Nonetheless, even if allowance is made for poetic licence, the scene drawn by the psalmist still demands an incredible miracle. For generations these people had been slaves, starved, beaten, and broken by their Egyptian masters. Oh! They were a sick, bruised, and feeble people! But now in a tremendous surge of divine mercy, of awesome power, at the very hour when the angel of death was striking the remainder of the land of Egypt, God banished from his people every trace of their servitude. By a superb miracle he caused them to begin their march to freedom as a dynamic, healthy, triumphant host. They numbered possibly two million [21] – a vast multitude. Yet at the time of the exodus they were either completely, or at least substantially free of disease!

Had they gone on to observe every commandment of the Lord, and to trust his promise and power, disease would have remained foreign to them. But they fell back from the Lord, and it was not long before many thousands of them were again bowed beneath the yoke of sickness and pain. But that unhappy relapse cannot alter the splendour of their initial period of divine health. Nor can it undo the terrific witness this miracle provides of the Lord's desire to bring all of his people out of an "Egyptian" bondage to sin and sickness, and into radiant life and strength.

(21) The book of *Numbers* indicates that the tribes could muster 603,550 fighting men.

CHAPTER FIVE:

THE BASIS OF THE COVENANT

The basis of God's healing covenant with Israel was three-fold – *promise, law, atonement.*

PROMISE

Healing was not promised to Israel because the nation had any right to it. In fact they did nothing to deserve it. On the contrary, their constant sin merited only judgment and annihilation (cp. Ex 32:10; Nu 14:11-12; 16:44-45). However, the Lord God is full of compassion and mercy, and he greatly wished to restore to the people as much of paradise as they could receive in their present life. So he gave them a promise of healing and of good health.

That promise was neither earned nor deserved. Each Israelite could personally procure it only by the exercise of faith.

The promise was left with Israel, but tragically *"the message which they heard did not benefit them, because it did not meet with faith in the hearers"* (He 4:1-2).

Here then is the simple answer to why the healing covenant was so largely ineffective throughout Israel's history. It was not that the promise had no value, nor that God was unwilling or unable to honour it, but only that neither prophet nor priest were able to persuade the people to believe it! The promise always remained with them, but they failed to reach it. The scripture is emphatic: *"For (only) we who have believed enter that rest"* (He 4:3).

To Israel the promise was given; to Israel the promise was preached; but for Israel the promise was not often performed. Against them the indictment is written: *"They were unable to enter because of unbelief"* (3:19). What was the cause of that unbelief? The answer is given very succinctly in *Hebrews 3:7-19* –

1) *__they hardened their hearts__* and rebelled against the will of God, provoking and embittering the Lord by their behaviour (vs. 8,10).

Nothing is more destructive of faith than apostasy! And apostasy begins when a man closes his ears and hardens his heart against the voice of God. So the admonition is thrice repeated: *"Therefore, as the Holy Spirit says, 'Today, when you hear his voice, do not harden your hearts!'"* (3:7,15; 4:7). And the apostle adds his own words: *"Take care, brethren, lest there be in any of you an evil unbelieving heart, leading you to fall away from the living God . . . For we share in Christ, if only we hold our first confidence firm to the end"* (3:12, 14).

2) ***they erred in their understanding*** of the ways of God (vs. 9). Because the Lord often moved slowly in the face of sin, because he was silent and reluctant in judgment, they thought he was as unrighteous as they were themselves (cp. Ps 50:21).

This failure to penetrate beyond the seeming indifference of heaven to a discovery of the divine compassion (which leads God to delay judgment in the hope of repentance) caused the people to ignore God and to reject his statutes. They did not understand his compassion, nor realise his kindness, nor honour his promise of blessing. Had they better understood the ways of the Lord they would not have gone astray in their hearts; but as it was, he was constrained to swear a terrible oath: *"They shall never enter into my rest!"* (He 3:10-11). They left their bones bleaching in the wilderness.

3) ***they departed from the living God*** (vs. 12). Through the deceitfulness of sin their hearts became hardened, and they were no longer able to perceive the presence of God or accept the validity of his promise.

It was inevitable that sickness and death should pursue them and overwhelm them.

Now a promise has been left to us, as it was to them: let us therefore take care lest we too, in hardness of heart, or in ignorance of God's power, even so much as seem to come short of it! (He 4:1,11). Rather, let us mix faith with the preaching and hearing of the promise, so there may be a full performance of every word God has spoken.

LAW

Conditions were laid against the promise that had to be met before the Lord would perform it. This was reasonable, for the promise was not given to enable people to live in sin. The same principle applies to the new covenant given to us in Christ (see Ja 5:16: 1 Co 11:29-30; Mt 5:23-24; Mk 11:24-26).

There are two aspects to those conditions: (1) violation of the provision of the covenant may lead to an infliction of its various penalties, which include sickness; (2) conformity to the provisions of the covenant creates a situation where it becomes proper for God to unleash its blessings.

This, then, is the only sense in which God can be strictly said to be the author of sickness and disease –

- he has established the law of sowing and reaping (Ga 6:7-8)
- he has ordained punishment for wrongdoing
- he permits, even causes, illness to fall as a penalty upon the disobedient.

But the root source of disease is sin and the virulent malice of Satan. It was never God's desire that people should be sick (Is 33:24).

However, it must be stressed again, that does not mean all sickness, or even most sickness, is an act of divine judgment. Many illnesses result simply from natural causes such as faulty diet, exposure to infection, unwise living habits, and so on. At other times, disease may spring from the oppression of Satan (Ac 10:38). But there are certainly some occasions when sickness is the penalty for violation of the law of God. In those cases God may be said to be the

- *author* of sickness, since he has decreed it as part of the general curse that has fallen upon man because of sin; and the
- a**gent** of sickness, in two ways: *(a) passively*, by removing his protection and leaving man defenceless against the onslaughts of disease and/or the devil; *(b) actively*, by commissioning his *"angel"* to do so (cp. 2 Sa 24:15-17; 1 Ch 21:14-15; 2 Kg 19:35; Is 37:36).

However, these acts of judgment are fundamentally alien to God, they are his *"strange work"*; he finds *"no pleasure in the death of the wicked"*, or for that matter "in the death of any one"; rather, his plea is, *"Why will you die? . . . Turn to me and LIVE!"* (Is 28:21; Ez 18:23,32; 33:11).

The Father's natural work is not to destroy but to save, not to afflict but to heal, not to slay but to make alive! Throughout the Bible, from Genesis to Revelation, his invitation is unchanged: *"Humble yourselves, pray, seek my face, turn from your wicked ways, then will I hear from heaven, I will forgive your sin, I will heal you."* (cp. 2 Ch 7:14).

ATONEMENT

Keeping the commandments of God was an essential condition for gaining health and prosperity. But that simple statement at once placed all people in bondage to disease and death, *"as it is written, none is righteous, no, not one . . . in their path are ruin and misery, and the way of peace they do not know"* (Ro 3:10-18).

Great though the promise was, the law placed us all under sin and effectively prevented us from obtaining the goodness of God. To meet this need the Lord in grace and mercy provided a method of atonement, by which he could justly and legally heed our cry and bring us deliverance.

Healing in the Bible is always closely linked with atonement, for unless God is able to provide a way to remove our sin, the law will always stand between us and the fulfilment of the promise. There is no conceivable way for us to provide a ransom for our own lives (cp. Ps 49:7-8), so it remained for the mercy of God to provide for us a full redemption. Because the Lord has done just that, he is able to extend his favour to the sick and to loose them from their infirmities.

Atonement is achieved by offering a suitable ransom, a substitutionary sacrifice whose life is offered in place of the life of the sinner. Without such a ransom, God could not in justice heal the sick; but the ransom enables God to satisfy the claims of his holy law, and also to fulfil the demands of his eternal love. Once the ransom has been paid, and atonement made, there is no legal reason why healing should be withheld. Offended righteousness has been placated. The way is now made open for the loving kindness of God to bring health to those who suffer. The one thing now required is that the afflicted show implicit faith in God's redemptive act, that they claim their legal rights, and take authority against the trespass of Satan in their lives.

This coupling of atonement with forgiveness of sin and healing is stressed in both Old and New Testaments. Here we shall consider only atonement in the old dispensation.

THE PASSOVER (EX 12:21-39)

This account reveals the first national atonement: it provided covering of the people's sin, protection from the wrath of God, and a marvellous work of healing. The blood of the sacrificial lambs, sprinkled on the doorways caused the Lord to pass over those houses and to protect the people from the angel of death. The lambs died in the place of the people. When the people showed their faith in God's promise by remaining within their houses, sheltered by the blood of the innocent sacrifices, the Lord was able to keep them from judgment and preserve them from the plague.

I have already indicated that a marvellous miracle of national healing took place as the people kept that first Passover feast. But it is worth noting also that this sweeping surge of divine healing was not restricted to the Israelites alone. A great number of Egyptians and other nationalities joined the exodus: *"a mixed multitude also went up with them,"* and they were included in the breathtaking paean, *"there was not one feeble person among all their tribes!"*

Those foreigners were people who had come to fear the Lord, who obeyed his command to prepare for a pilgrimage, and who took shelter with Israel beneath the sprinkled blood. For them too, the blood provided atonement, and in that atonement they found pardon, healing, and a place in the kingdom of God.

Still another example of the Passover sacrifice bringing healing to the people is found in the story of Hezekiah who *"prayed for them saying, 'The good Lord pardon everyone who sets his heart to seek God'. . . and the Lord heard Hezekiah and healed the people."* (2 Ch 30:13-20)

ATONEMENT PREVENTING PLAGUE (NU 8:18-19)

The Levites were especially appointed by God to work in the tabernacle and to make atonement for the people as they came to worship the Lord. Only by this service could Israel be kept free of the condemnation of sin and from the curse of disease; only by this means was it possible for the Lord to dwell among the people in mercy and blessing. Again we see the close connection between sin and sickness; and again we see that unless atonement was made to cover the nation's sin the people were subject to the wrath of God and left open to many dread plagues.

In several places reports are given of an outbreak of plague caused by sin; and in each case the progress of the epidemic was stopped only when proper atonement was made (see Nu 16:46-48; 25:1-13; 2 Sa 24:18-25). On each of those occasions the people were healed, not because their moral condition was improved, but simply because adequate atonement turned aside the anger of God, so that he was able to demonstrate his mercy. Nevertheless, the atonement was certainly a symbol of sincere repentance on the part of many of the people, and it was joined with at least some effort by the whole nation once again to obey the law of God.

To state it another way: the people gained healing solely on the legal and redemptive basis of atonement; but it was expected that their faith in, and appropriation of, the values of the atonement would be followed by a renewed desire to live righteously before God. Without such a desire their faith would be quickly nullified, and they would again become easy prey for the malice of Satan.

THE CURE FOR LEPROSY (LE 14:1-7; DE 24:8-9)

Lepers were especially commanded to observe the laws of atonement and cleansing; and the example of Miriam was cited to remind them that God has power both to cause the affliction and to cure it. There is a warning and a promise here –

- a warning that disobedience and unbelief will strengthen disease

- a promise that repentance, faith, and obedience to God's command can bring recovery.

The instructions in *Leviticus 14:1* ff. relate specifically to a leper who had been already healed of his leprosy; but Christ's use of this law indicates that it was assumed the cure had come from God (see Mt 8:4; Lu 5:12-14). The ceremony of cleansing in fact did contain many elements that typified the healing covenant God had made with Israel and also foreshadowed the atonement made by Christ.

For example, Finis Dake writes –

(The sevenfold sprinkling) symbolised the completeness and perfection of the remedy, and foreshadowed the removal of all sin, sickness, pain, and suffering through Jesus Christ . . . The living and the dead birds typified the death and resurrection of Christ through which sin, sickness, and the entire curse would be removed from mankind. They also pictured the leper freed from sin, sickness, and suffering to go free and walk in newness of life in perfect deliverance from his curse, enjoying salvation and health, fellowship with his own kind, and communion with Jehovah.[22]

OTHER EXAMPLES

Other examples of atonement bringing healing are found in the story of *the brass serpent*, and in the prophecies of *Isaiah*. You will find a study of them in the companion volume to this one, which deals with atonement and healing in the New Testament.

(22) The Dake Annotated Reference Bible; Dake Pub. Co. Inc.; Lawrenceville, Georgia, 1963.

CHAPTER SIX:

YAHWEH–RAPHA

T here are eight covenant names by which God revealed himself and
his purpose to Israel. These names comprehend all the benefits God
made available to Israel through his covenant; they show the full
measure of his love, and of his willingness to meet his people at each
point where their need was greatest.

These names express the extraordinary relationship God was willing to
enter into with those who worshipped him; they show the titles by which
he wished to be known; they identify his true character; they expose
those matters about which God was especially anxious the people should
pray.

Whoever knew those names, and called upon the God they represented,
had God's promise that he would behave toward them in the fashion
demanded by each of his titles. In every time of need the people could
address God by one or more of these titles, expecting that the Lord would
freely give them the benefits his names defined.

Here are these eight covenant names, listed in the order of their historical
revelation to Israel. [23]

THE COVENANT NAMES OF GOD

YAHWEH-JIREH.........the Lord our Provider (Ge 22:8,14).

---

(23) *Yahweh* is an English transliteration of the Hebrew personal name for God.
The Hebrew word, known as "the tetragrammaton", consisted only of four
consonants YHWH. The ancient Jews treated this divine name as too holy
to pronounce, and usually substituted another title for it when they read the
scriptures, with the result the true pronunciation has become lost. Around
the 12th cent. A.D., the vowels "e", "o", and "a" were added to give
Jehovah; but many scholars now reckon that the form Yahweh is closer to
the original.

YAHWEH-RAPHA ....the Lord our Healer (Ex 15:26).
YAHWEH-NISSI ....the Lord our Banner (Ex 17:15).
YAHWEH-QADESH ....the Lord our Sanctifier (Le 20:8; Ez 20:12)
YAHWEH-SHALOM...........the Lord our Peace (Jg 6:24).
YAHWEH-RAAH................the Lord our Shepherd (Ps 23:1).
YAHWEH-TSIDKENU ....the Lord our Righteousness (Je 23:6)
YAHWEH-SHAMMAH.......the Lord Ever Present (Ez 48:35).

Yahweh is peculiarly the personal name by which the Lord God revealed himself to Israel. It stands in contrast with other more or less impersonal titles by which God was also known – e.g. *Elohim, Adonai, El Elyon.* Yahweh was especially used to express the personal covenant the Lord God had entered into with Israel.

Yahweh means "Eternal". Its full significance is displayed in the words, *"he called upon the name of the Lord* (Yahweh)*, the Everlasting God"* (Ge 21:33). And again, *"God said to Moses, I AM WHO I AM,"* (or, *"I WILL BE WHAT I WILL BE"*) (Ex 3:13-14) And again, *"I am the Alpha and the Omega, says the Lord God, who is and who was and who is to come, the Almighty"* (Re 1:8).

But if *Yahweh* means the *God who is Eternal*, it also means the God who is the *Same Forever – "I am Yahweh, I change not!"* (Ma 3:6). Can that mean anything less than this: what God was to Israel in the past, he is today? He is the eternal, unchanging, covenant-keeping God (De 7:9). Having given his oath, he will never violate it (He 6:17-18). He must still be today all that is revealed in his covenant names of old.

The Yahweh who promised then cannot dismiss his promise now, for the very linking of Yahweh with the promise shows that the promise is as eternal as the name!

The only change that has overtaken the promise is its enlargement beyond Israel to embrace the entire human race. The Lord Jesus Christ, to whom the name Yahweh now rightly belongs (for *Jesus* means *Yahweh our Saviour*), has accomplished this. And of him it is said, *"Jesus Christ is the same yesterday and today and for ever"* (He 13:8). Christ has made the full extent of the promise available to any person who believes.

THE BLESSINGS PROMISED

The fact that the promises belong to an eternal covenant is shown by the union of Yahweh with the promises; but the nature of the promises themselves is shown by the graphic adjectives and nouns linked with Yahweh. Examination of the eight compound titles given to God in scripture shows that the Lord has entered into an everlasting commitment to

- provide our daily needs
- go before us in all the battles of life
- sanctify and make us holy
- give us peace
- shepherd us in times of pleasantness and of sorrow
- give us his own righteousness
- remain by our side for all eternity, and
- to be our Great Physician.

Now all sincere Christians gladly accept seven of those gracious benefits. We know that God was in fact all of those things to Israel in the past, and that Christ is all of those things to us today. But many Christian people ignore the eighth: Yahweh-RAPHA, *"the Lord our Healer"* – or at least, they ignore its literal application and think only in terms of spiritual, not physical healing.

Yet the appellation Rapha is just as emphatic as any of the others. The statement, *"the Lord our Healer,"* is no less certain than *"the Lord our Righteousness,"* or *"the Lord our Peace."* If I may still literally say, *"The Lord is my Shepherd, I shall not want,"* then I can just as surely say, *"The Lord is my Healer, I shall be made whole."*

If it is still legitimate to believe that Yahweh-Shammah will never leave us nor forsake us, then it is equally lawful to affirm that Yahweh-Rapha will still act as our Great Physician!

If his name is Yahweh, then we are compelled to believe that our God is forever the same. If he has linked Yahweh with his promise, then we must also accept that his promise is forever the same. The promise and the name, linked together, reveal the eternal character of God.

The conclusion seems unavoidable: just as it has always been Yahweh's nature to pardon the sin of his people, so it is always his nature to heal their sickness.

THE PROMISE ENRICHED IN CHRIST

The New Testament makes it plain that Christ assumed the responsibility of fulfilling to his church all the blessings of the covenant God had made with Israel

Two things appear –

"JESUS" IS SYNONYMOUS WITH "YAHWEH"

"Jesus" is an anglicised form of the Greek transliteration of the ordinary Hebrew name "Joshua", or "Jehoshua" = Yahweh-is-Saviour. This was (and is) a common name for Hebrew boys; but since it was given to Mary's baby by specific command of the archangel, it plainly held for this Boy a much deeper significance. He was to be called Yahweh-is-Saviour because it would be HE who would *"save his people from their sins"* (Mt 1:21).

John gives further confirmation of this identification of Jesus with Yahweh. The apostle declares that when Isaiah saw a magnificent vision of Yahweh in his Temple (Is 6:1-10), it was actually a vision of the Lord Jesus Christ *"in his glory"* (Jn 12:37-41).

Can it be doubted any longer that the covenant name Yahweh plainly belongs to Christ?

THE COMPOUND TITLES BELONG TO CHRIST

It can be easily shown that each one of the compound titles of God is applicable to Christ, hence the promises they contain are freely available to us –

Yahweh-JIREH .... Ph 4:19
Yahweh-RAPHA .... 1 Pe 2:24
Yahweh-NISSI .... Jn 10:4
Yahweh-QADESH .... 1 Co 1:30
Yahweh-SHALOM .... Ep 2:14

Yahweh-RAAH .... Jn 10:11
Yahweh-TSIDKENU .... Ph 3:9
Yahweh-SHAMMAH .... Mt 28:20

Can there be any doubt that the covenant name Yahweh-RAPHA is as much our right as ever it was that of ancient Israel? And not merely our right, but more richly our right – for the promise that comes to us through CHRIST is immeasurably better than that given to Israel through MOSES!

YAHWEH – RAPHA

The compound title Yahweh-Rapha is found in *Exodus 15:23-26*. From that passage we can learn –

1)   The promise contained in this name definitely refers to the cure of physical illness, for the Lord said, *"I will put none of the diseases upon you that I have put upon the Egyptians, for I am the Lord (Yahweh) your Healer (Rapha)."*

2)   God intended this incident at Marah to be a parable to Israel. They had just escaped from Egypt, which typified the world of sin. Now they were on their journey through the wilderness toward Canaan, which spoke of the passage of life. On the way, they thirsted and came to Marah, the place of bitter waters – a picture of the interludes of suffering that come into every life. But when Moses prayed, the Lord answered at once, and showed him that a tree cast into the pool would make the bitter sweet. God then turned this into an occasion for introducing to Israel both a statute and an ordinance of healing.

We Christians cannot avoid seeing in this tree a picture of the cross of the Lord Jesus Christ. Once let the tree of Calvary be brought to bear upon a life made bitter with the anguish of sin or sickness, and healing must inevitably follow, the fountain of life will again be made sweet.

But two things are necessary: as he did with Moses, God must first open our eyes, so that he can show us the healing power inherent in Calvary;

then we must take up the cross and boldly cast it upon the bitter waters of our pain. Only then will healing come. [24]

I am saying simply, God cannot withhold healing when a person claims it in full compliance with the covenant (his own promise binds him to fulfil that covenant); and normally, failure to adhere to the requirements of the covenant will mean loss of the promised benefit.

But obviously, God can, if he pleases, show mercy and miracle to any person, whether or not they are obeying his command – although, again, his justice will ultimately demand that punishment must fall upon those who are continually disobedient and unrepentant.

3) *"There Yahweh made for them a statute and an ordinance."* While those two expressions are almost synonymous, it would be fair to say that "statute" refers to the written aspect of the law, but "ordinance" refers to the action that follows the keeping of the law.

In the case before us,

- **the statute is**, *"Hearken to the voice of the Lord your God, and do that which is right in his eyes, and give heed to his commandments and keep all his statutes;"* while

- **the ordinance is**, *"I will put none of the diseases upon you which I put upon the Egyptians, for I am the Lord your healer."*

---

(24) For the sake of simplicity, clarity, and emphasis, I am obliged to use more or less absolute expressions such as this one: "only then will healing come." It should be realised that behind all such expressions lies a recognition that *"our God is in the heavens, and he does whatever he pleases . . . the Lord is great . . . whatever the Lord pleases he does, in heaven and on earth"* (Ps 115:3; 135:6). In other words, God is sovereign, and while he cannot refuse to honour his promise he is certainly free to go beyond it.

Hence, my phrase, and others like it throughout these lessons, should be read as though it said: "Normally, healing will come only when these conditions are fulfilled. But of course God is free to act in mercy and to heal a sick person, if he so chooses, even when the terms of the covenant have not been properly fulfilled."

The *statute* is the divine enactment, while the *ordinance* is the benefit conferred by adherence to the statute.

The point of the argument is this: God has laid upon us the same statute as he laid on Israel, therefore it is reasonable to suppose that the attached ordinance is also the same. We are no less obliged than they were to listen to the commandments God has given us, and to obey. Are we then to be less privileged than they in the promise associated with obedience? It is fairer to believe that since the statute is the same for us, so also is the ordinance.

4)   God gave a powerful declaration of his eternal healing nature when he called himself Yahweh-Rapha. The statement can be analysed as follows–

I AM – God must always speak of himself in the present tense, for he dwells in eternity, not time; with him there are no yesterdays or tomorrows. He is always the great I AM, the eternal, unchanging God.

I AM THE LORD – the introduction of his personal name, Yahweh, at once defines what he is about to say concerning his covenant: that covenant will be as eternal, as unchanging, as efficacious as the God who makes it.

I AM THE LORD YOUR HEALER – here the promise is identified as a covenant of healing, and it is made personal to us. He is not Yahweh-Rapha in heaven, for in heaven there is no sickness. He is not Yahweh-Rapha to the world at large, for the world neither obeys nor worships him. He is YOUR Healer. That is, the promise is to you who hear his voice, who know his covenant, who have embraced his word, who accept the redemption and deliverance he freely offers. Only to the people of the covenant is God known by his name "Yahweh-Rapha". The warm and personal relationship of Physician is not given to those who spurn his love or ignore his voice! But to YOU who hear and heed, he is "THE LORD YOUR HEALER".

CHAPTER SEVEN:

MANY MIRACLES

Here is a chronicle of disease and, in some instances, of supernatural healing, as recorded in the general history of Israel after the nation was settled in Canaan.

HANNAH AND SAMUEL (1 SA 1:1-20)

"The Lord had closed her womb;" so the scripture says twice (vs. 5,6); from which we learn that God may cause or allow an infirmity to grip us so that we might be drawn, as Hannah was, to seek the Lord in prayer.

But notice that the affliction itself brought no blessing; on the contrary it was a source of deep unhappiness, and it is perhaps sad that Hannah waited so many years before she found faith to pray for the Lord to heal her. Yet her need did drive her to a place of passionate desire and of total consecration to the Lord. The result, when she did finally call upon God for deliverance, was a swift answer. Her request was granted and she gained the miracle she desired.

A similar situation may still arise today where people are unaware of, or have forgotten God's covenant of healing. But the example of Hannah shows that while God could make use of an infirmity to gain Samuel for the service of the Temple, the sickness itself brought him no glory; rather, it was a source of vexation and shame. The greatest honour came to the Lord and the sweetest happiness to Hannah only when she prayed for and gained healing.

JEREBOAM'S WITHERED HAND (1 KG 13:1-6)

When Jereboam tried to arrest the bold prophet who pronounced a curse on the king's altar, the Lord struck the monarch and withered his hand. God may at times send sickness as a judgment for sin. But just as promptly, when the king humbled himself and repented, and desired the prophet to pray for his restoration, the Lord showed him mercy and his hand was made quite whole.

ELIJAH AND THE WIDOW'S SON (1 KG 17:17-24)

See how the woman instantly connected her son's disease with her sin, and how she accused the prophet of bringing this judgment against her. Elijah did not know whether or not the woman's sin was the cause of her sorrow, so he gave her no answer, but silently carried the lad to his bed. Yet he did recognise this tragedy as an evil, he knew it could not bring glory to God for the boy to die, and so he cried passionately for the Lord to restore him to life. *"The Lord heard the voice of Elijah, and the soul of the child came into him again."*

At once the woman saw the significance of this great miracle, and she exclaimed, *"Now by this I know that you are a man of God, and that the word of the Lord in your mouth is truth!"* This woman showed instinctive recognition of two things:

- *"the word of the Lord"* is essentially a healing word, its presence is revealed by the healing it brings; and

- a ministry of healing by the word of the Lord is a mark of the true man of God.

It is a pity that awareness of these two things has become so dim today.

AHAZIAH AND THE SOLDIERS (2 KG 1:9-17).

The death of Ahaziah and his soldiers is a sobering reminder of God's ability to destroy in anger, as well as to save in mercy. Those who died did so because they were haughty, unrepentant, and had no fear of God: those who lived were spared because they showed proper humility and faith.

Similar incidents are recorded in the New Testament, which we shall consider in their place (Ac 5:1-11; 13:6-11); but it is also noteworthy that when the disciples recalled Elijah calling down fire from heaven and desired to do the same, Christ rebuked them (Lu 9:51-56). He said he had come, *"not to destroy men's lives but to save them"*. In other words, it is still possible for God to stretch out his hand in judgment, but the overwhelming emphasis in this present day is deliverance, not destruction.

ELISHA AND THE WATERS OF JERICHO (2 KG 2:19-22)

Elisha sweetened the brackish waters of Jericho and once again gave a marvellous demonstration of God's willingness to turn barrenness into pleasantness. Once again we can see another dramatic picture of the gospel. "Jericho" signifies the world; "the people of the city" are those servants of God who find the world barren and dry. Elisha is a type of Christ. The new bowl and the salt represent the new covenant of deliverance wrought by Jesus at Calvary. When it is cast upon the springs of human life, the gospel brings healing, it breaks the power of death, and it makes the barren heart a fruitful garden!

ELISHA AND THE SHUNAMMITE'S SON (2 KG 4:8-17)

Elisha and the woman from Shunam provide a charming example of God's great willingness to give their heart's desires to those who delight themselves in him and serve him well (Ps 37:4). In this case the woman desired healing for herself, so that a son might be born to her. She hardly dared to believe it could be done; but the Lord marked her devoted service, and abundantly met her longing.

THE SHUNAMMITES'S SON RESTORED (2 KG 4:18-37)

The healing of the widow's son by Elijah many years before now bore fruit in the faith of the Shunammite. When her boy died she apparently remembered the story of what Elijah had done and she laid her child on Elisha's bed, saying, *"It shall be well"*. She then hurried off to get Elisha, having no doubt the prophet could call upon his God and restore the boy to life. And so it happened.

ELISHA NEUTRALISING THE POTTAGE (2 KG 4:38-44)

The two miracles here – removing the poison from the broth, and multiplying the loaves – are a further object lesson of God's desire to rid our lives of all the venom of sin and sickness, and to meet our every need. Note that the people, who were quite happy to eat the previously poisoned broth once the prophet had declared it safe, matched the faith of Elisha. There was a famine in the land, but that did not prevent God from providing abundantly for his servants, even though it required a miracle of healing.

NAAMAN AND GEHAZI (2 KG 5:1-27)

The case of Naaman is a striking example of the natural recognition given to the healing ministry of the prophets in old Israel. The little girl had no doubt God could heal Naaman if he would only visit Elisha. Even the craven king of Israel recognised it was the prerogative of God *"to kill and to make alive"*, although he evidently had not a shred of real faith.

Elisha, however, calmly took control and requested the king to send leprous Naaman to him, declaring that the Lord would heal the captain. So it happened, according to the word of the prophet, and in response also to the humility and faith of Naaman. The result was Naaman's immediate recognition of the Lord as the only true God. The deceit and greed of Gehazi, however, were punished, for he was stricken with leprosy. In the healing of the one we can find a promise; but in the affliction of the other we find a warning. [25]

ELISHA AND THE BLIND SYRIANS (2 KG 6:15-23)

This astonishing miracle provides vivid evidence of God's power to afflict or to heal. It shows his judgment on sin and on those who seek to harm his servants; and it reveals also that God does not destroy unnecessarily – he is willing rather to show mercy and deliverance.

---

(25) Gehazi's appearance later, still as Elisha's servant (2 Kg 8:4) has caused some difficulty among commentators. Three main solutions are offered

- the chronological order of the stories about Elisha and Gehazi has become confused, so that the incident recorded in 2 Kg. 8:1-6 actually occurred before Gehazi was stricken with leprosy.

- because Gehazi's leprosy had rapidly reached the stage of turning his skin white he was no longer "unclean", and could therefore continue in Elisha's service (cp. 2 Kg. 5:27 with Le 13:12,13).

- despite Elisha's pronouncement that the leprosy would "cleave" to him "for ever", Gehazi had repented, cried out to God for mercy, and had been healed.

THE DEAD MAN AND ELISHA'S BONES (2 KG 13:20-21)

How strongly the Lord God wants to prove himself the Great Physician! If he cannot find a living prophet's hands through which to channel his power, he will use a dead prophet's bones! But one way or another God will demonstrate his willingness to heal. It may be argued that all of Elisha's former miracles were wrought by God merely to prove that he was a prophet. But this miracle, wrought long after Elisha's death, shows the true purpose of all these signs and wonders. They were wrought

- to confirm, not the prophet, but the WORD OF GOD spoken by the prophet – a purpose that is still served by miracles of healing; and

- to confirm the nature of God as *"the Lord your Healer"*.

And in times when God can find no preacher faithful enough to declare his true Word, he may work an exceptional and dramatic sign, like the restoration of this dead man, to prove that the Great Physician is ever the same!

A SUN-DIAL AND A POULTICE (2 KG 20:1-11; IS 38:1-22)

Hezekiah, the king of Judah, gives us a fascinating example of healing in the Old Testament –

1)   Hezekiah was a young man, about 40 years of age, and he could not accept that it was God's will for him to die at the prime of life and service (Is 38:10). He rejected Isaiah's word that this was God's doing (2 Kg 20:1), and at once set himself to reverse the decree and gain healing. He recognised that his death could bring no gain to him, nor any glory to God (Is 38: 18-19). But recovery would be a source of abounding happiness and a testimony of God's mighty power and mercy (vs. 17,20).

2)   He remembered God's covenant with Israel at the waters of Marah (Ex 15:26), and claimed he had a right to healing because he had kept the statutes of the Lord (2 Kg 20:3).

3)   He knew the power of fervent, sincere, prayer to move the hand of God to great exploits (vs. 2-5; and compare Ja 5:16).

4)   He did not deny the use of natural remedies to facilitate recovery (vs. 7).

5)   In great boldness of faith he asked God for a special sign to prove that he would fully recover (as Isaiah had said) in the remarkably short time of three days. So, to prove his willingness to heal just one man, the Lord God disturbed the majestic course of the entire heavens, and wrought a miracle that staggered the whole earth! Ambassadors even came from far away Babylon to inquire of Hezekiah the cause of this stupendous disarray of heaven! (2 Ch 32:31). [26]

6)   This incident is a powerful demonstration of the reality of divine healing. It shows that God does not finally want his people to be sick, nor to be cut off in their prime (except when, as in the case of David's son, sickness is sent as an irreversible judgment on sin). And it shows that when the right conditions are found healing can be snatched from the very jaws of death. What are those conditions? Such qualities as deep repentance and humility, fervent prayer, and unshakable faith. [27]

---

(26) I have assumed here that the alteration in the motion of the shadow presupposes an alteration in the motion of either the sun or the earth, or perhaps both. It should be noted though that scripture mentions only that the shadow receded; nothing is said about the cause of this recession. Some commentators think the miracle involved only the movement of that particular shadow, and only one sun-dial, not any others; in other words, no planetary disruption was involved.

In either case the question still arises, whether the retreat of the shadow was wholly supernatural or involved some natural cause? The question cannot be resolved, except to say

- in the Bible the description of an event as a "miracle" does not preclude the idea that God may have used natural means.

- the supernatural aspect of an event may lie in its timing and in the results it produces rather than in the phenomenon itself.

- there may be an intermingling of natural and supernatural causes.

The possibility of a great disruption of the planetary system being the cause of Hezekiah's retreating shadow was graphically described by Dr. Immanuel Velikovsky, in his book Worlds In Collision; Victor Gollancz Ltd., London; 1952.

(27) It is probable that recognition of this idea underlies Hezekiah's words in 2 Kg 20:19 and Is 39:8 −"Why not, if there will be peace and security in my days?" At first sight that statement seems callous and cynical, as though

. . . continued on next page.

ASA AND HIS GOUT (2 CH 16:12-13)

The indictment of Asa is blunt and tragic – "in his disease he did not seek the Lord, but sought help from physicians." The result was inevitable – "Asa died."

The most unhappy aspect of Asa's experience is that in almost every other respect he was a man of sincere faith and devotion to the Lord. Actually, his very name "Asa" in the Hebrew tongue means "healing"; yet, while he was zealous for the Lord, his faith seems to have fallen short of believing in God's supernatural intervention.

The Bible says, "Asa did that which was right in the eyes of the Lord" and his "heart was wholly true to the Lord all his days" (1 Kg 15:9-15). Yet there was a weakness in his faith, a hesitancy to trust himself wholly to God's supernatural power. This fault showed itself in his failure to remove some of the idolatrous high places (1 Kg 15:14) in his carnal league with the king of Syria (2 Ch 16:1-10), and in his absolute reliance upon physicians rather than upon the healing power of God (2 Ch 16:12-13).

Many years before his death Asa's weakness was recognised by the Lord, and a prophet was commissioned to go and warn the king. In view of Asa's later failure, the prophet's words are quite pointed: "The Lord is with you, while you are with him; if you seek him, he will be found by you; but if you forsake him, he will forsake you . . . but you, take courage! Do not let your hands be weak" (2 Ch 15:2,7). In the matter of his disease Asa forsook the Lord, or at least, he placed all his trust in his doctors and did not seek healing from God, so he died. The scripture, of course, does not condemn the doctors, nor was there any wrong in seeking medical help. The fault lay in Asa's total reliance on medicine and his lack of faith in God's healing power.

. . . continued from previous page.

Hezekiah cared nothing for his children so long as his own skin was safe. But that seems too much out of character. His meaning was probably: "My own experience has shown me how good God's word is, and how merciful he is. Just as he has turned my judgment into peace and security, because I repented, so I am sure he will do the same for my descendants if they also repent." Unhappily, they did not repent, and the nation was destroyed.

The experience of Asa provides a simple answer to those who point to fine Christian people who are sick, saying that these people would surely be healed if it was God's will for them to be made whole. But Asa was a godly man, loved by God (2 Ch 15:17) and loved by all the people (2 Ch 16:14); a man who, despite occasional faults, served righteousness throughout his life. Yet because he failed to trust the healing promise, because he did not believe God was able and willing to cure him, he suffered an agonising disease, which finally took his life.

Had he sought healing from God at the onset of this affliction it presumably would never have become "exceeding great", he would have been restored, and would have gained (as Hezekiah did) many more years of active service for the Lord.

So the lesson is plain: great faith in God, and great zeal for the scriptures, will not prevent disease from overtaking us unless we also have a specific and definite faith in the Bible promise of healing and in God's ability and willingness to deliver us from every affliction. Without such faith, the life of the choicest saint may be too soon stricken down, and their service cut short.

CHAPTER EIGHT:
HE STORY OF JOB – (I)

THE GREAT DEBATE

D o yourself a favour. Put this book down, open your Bible, and read right through the book of *Job*. Read it twice, three times, and then again – in different translations if you have them. Nothing I can write will teach you as much as will the book itself. You will discover in *Job* not only some of the most superb poetry that has ever been written, but also some of the most profound explorations of man's relationships with the providence of God. [28]

OUTLINE OF THE BOOK

PROLOGUE

Job begins with a section of prose, recording Job's character, the permission given to Satan to afflict him, and the series of disasters that befell him (1:1-2:13). From this point the remainder of the book is superb poetry, apart from a final brief section of prose in the epilogue

---

(28) I will make no attempt to comment on matters such as the authorship of *Job*, the date of its composition, its historicity, etc. For the purpose of this study I am simply accepting the book as it stands, with the single exception of emending the text to identify Zophar as the speaker in 27:7-23.

Not all scholars agree with this emendation. But many do hold the view that Job could not have spoken the words in that passage because otherwise they would represent the patriarch as suddenly and inexplicably adopting the creed of his friends – that is, that Job's afflictions resulted from personal sin.

As one scholar writes: "We have no parallel to these verses in Job's speeches in any other part of the book. On the other hand, the passage would sound perfectly in place on the lips of the friends." Attributing the speech to Zophar means that, like Eliphaz and Bildad, he also has three speeches.

(42:7-17). Most modern translations clearly show the poetic structure of the greater part of the book. It is worthwhile to remember that this middle section, being poetry, is rich in hyperbole and figurative allusions, which characterise poetic form. It ought not to be read as sober history.

THE GREAT DEBATE

Most of the book is devoted to the debate between Job and his three friends, with a final speech by a young man called Elihu. Then suddenly: the voice of God speaks out of a whirlwind; Job and his friends are compelled to repent of their foolishness; and Job's prosperity is restored.

The debate is divided into three trilogies. In each trilogy Job speaks three times, and each of the friends replies to him. Then Job speaks once more, followed by Elihu. Job has no reply to offer Elihu.

C. J. Ellicott characterises the friends thus:

> Eliphaz was the poet and spiritual man, who sees visions, and dreams dreams; Bildad was the man who rested on authority and appealed to tradition; Zophar was the man of worldly wisdom and common sense. [29]

J. S. Baxter describes Eliphaz as the voice of personal experience and inner illumination; Bildad as the voice of religious tradition and orthodoxy; Zophar as the voice of assumption and dogmatism –

Elihu stands by himself. Some reject him as a brash and conceited youth who spoke arrant nonsense. Others disagree. They suggest that while Elihu's attitude may seem bigoted to us, it was probably quite acceptable in its own setting. He showed humility and patience when he waited until his elders had exhausted their wisdom. My own inclination is to agree with those who accept Elihu's description of himself as a teacher inspired by God. Not that his teaching was infallible (God's personal appearance at the end of his speech indicates its shortcomings), but it spoke more truth than the others had spoken.

------

(29) I have lost the source of this quote.

The debate is divided thus –

> ### The first trilogy –
> Job's first speech (ch. 3)
> > Eliphaz answers (ch. 4 & 5)
> Job's second speech (ch. 6 & 7)
> > Bildad answers (ch. 8)
> Job's third speech (ch. 9 & 10)
> > Zophar answers (ch. 11)
>
> ### The second trilogy –
> Job's first speech (ch. 12,13,14)
> > Eliphaz answers (ch. 15)
> Job's second speech (ch. 16,17)
> > Bildad answers (ch. 18)
> Job's third speech (ch. 19)
> > Zophar answers (ch. 20)
>
> ### The third trilogy –
> Job's first speech (ch. 21)
> > Eliphaz answers (ch. 22)
> Job's second speech (ch. 23,24)
> > Bildad answers (ch. 25)
> Job's third speech (ch. 26;27:1-6)
> > Zophar answers (ch. 27:7-23)

Job's final speech
– *"The words of Job are ended"* (28,29,30,31)
– then follows a brief passage of prose introducing Elihu (32:1-5).

Elihu's speech (ch. 32-37)

The Lord speaks out of the whirlwind (ch. 38,39,40,41)

Job's final reply (42:1-6)

Epilogue (42:7-16)

G. Harding Wood writes –

> *Job* is the one book in the Bible concerned with what
> nowadays we call the "Problem of Pain". But there is
> very much more here than that. The writer faces the
> fundamental question: "How can we believe that God is
> love in face of the sufferings of mankind?" Is God really
> just, and if so, why do innocent people suffer? This
> problem is touched upon in some of the *Psalms* and in
> *Ecclesiastes*, but it is fully faced only in *Job*.
>
> In the prologue it is suggested that suffering is allowed
> by God as a test of our loyalty to him. In the speeches of
> Job's three friends . . . suffering is a judgment on sin. In
> the philosophy of Elihu, suffering is explained as a
> warning to the sinner. In the final revelation of God in
> the closing chapters, suffering is only one part of
> universal human experience; and that experience is not
> explained by God, and cannot be fully understood by us .
> . . The book opens with problems and questions, and
> ends with Job the sufferer silenced by a revelation of
> God. He does not find the answer he was seeking, but he
> loses the question he was asking. [30]

As the book of *Job* investigates these problems it raises several
paradoxes; and it is through these paradoxes that the real message of the
book is disclosed.

PARADOXES IN *JOB*

THE PROLOGUE AND EPILOGUE

A modern reader of *Job* finds one major problem of the book solved for
him by this simple fact: we know from the prologue that Satan was the
immediate cause of Job's suffering; and we know from the epilogue the

---

(30) Bird's-eye View of the Bible, Vol. 1; Marshall, Morgan, & Scott Ltd., London,
1957; pg. 104.

happy end of the story. Had Job and his friends known those things the great debate probably would never have taken place.

Instead, they were quite convinced God was the direct author of Job's miseries (3:23; 6:4; 7:12; etc.)

But does our favoured insight invalidate for us their debate, reducing it to a level of mere academic interest? Hardly, for in his revelation of himself to Job, God neither affirmed nor denied the charge that he had personally afflicted the patriarch. He simply ignored the charge. Job and his friends presumably died in ignorance of the dialogue that had occurred in heaven between Satan and God. The revelation of the spiritual background to the events was apparently given to some later author, perhaps the anonymous genius who put the story into its present form.

What does this paradox teach us? Essentially two things

- Satan may well be the actual author of the infirmities and sorrows that overtake our lives; but

- just as the human actors in Job's drama remained ignorant of Satan's involvement, so we are usually unable to discern whether or not he is present.

This allows us to speak in general terms about Satan as the source of our afflictions, but only rarely are we able to identify his presence in any specific situation. It is normally as true of us as it was of Job –

> (he was) not meant to know the explanation of his trial; and on this simple fact everything hangs. If Job had known, there would have been no place for faith; and the man could never have come forth as gold purified in the fire . . . the scriptures are as wise in their reservations as in their revelations. Enough is revealed to make faith intelligent. Enough is reserved to give faith scope for development. [31]

---

(31) J. Sidlow Baxter; Explore The Book, Vol. 3; Marshall, Morgan, & Scott, London, 1952; pg. 27.

For this reason we may find ourselves facing the same dilemma as Job, and enduring the same agony of doubt. A bewildered sufferer today may find in Job's anguish an echo of the cry in his own heart.

TWO CENTRAL QUESTIONS

On the surface, the main question raised in *Job* is the problem of pain. Yet closer examination of the book shows this is not the issue at all; in fact it is largely ignored. The real focus of *Job* is two-fold –

CAN PIETY SURVIVE WITHOUT PROSPERITY?

The story of Job begins with Satan's sneer: *"Does Job fear God for naught? . . . Put forth thy hand now, and touch all that he has, and he will curse thee to thy face"* (1:9,11). Whatever Job himself thought about his trials, it is evident that the author of the book considered this was the central (or at least the first) lesson to be learned: piety does not depend on prosperity; nor does piety always bring unbroken prosperity.

Satan asked, *"Does Job fear God for naught?"* He expected an answer in the negative, and, surprisingly, the three friends actually agreed with him. M. L. Chapman writes –

> Satan does not believe that Job will *"retain his integrity"* without a reward. The friends believe the material prosperity enjoyed by a man is the reward for integrity and that, therefore, the lack of reward is prima facie evidence of sin. The poet-author has Job come out as victor over these enemies. Satan is proved wrong because Job does not 'curse God' at the loss of health and wealth. Job defeats the friends in their contention. He argues persuasively from the realities of life that wealth and blessedness do not always result from righteousness . . . However, Job has not survived his trial without being marked by it . . . In defending his integrity he impugned the integrity of God . . . It is this issue to which God addresses himself. He does not enter into a

judicial dispute with Job, but shows him the true relationship that must always exist between God and man. [32]

The paradox in this situation arises because the first part of the prologue does in fact indicate a very definite link between piety and prosperity; and so does the epilogue. In fact some commentators have felt that the epilogue is so discontinuous with the major argument of the book that it must be a later and spurious addition by an inferior writer. But Chapman comments:

> Job has spent much of his time denying that material prosperity is the reward of righteousness. Therefore to have the book end with the Lord giving Job *"twice as much as he had before"* (42:10) seems incongruous . . . However . . . the real purpose of the author is simply to maintain that a man can be good without being rewarded for it. It is at this point that Job is the victor. He accepts both good and ill from God without rebelling against him, even though he does ask why, and sometimes bitterly assumes that God is against him without cause. Job did not demand restoration of his prosperity as a condition for serving God. That which he asked was a vindication of his character. When this is achieved it is not inconsistent with the author's purpose and argument to permit the narrative to have a materially happy ending for Job. [33]

The lesson is twofold –

- while the prologue and epilogue truly show a general link between piety and prosperity, the remainder of the book shows that the link is not absolute. In the special providence of God

---

(32) <u>Beacon Bible Commentary</u>, Vol. 3; pg. 22; Beacon Hill Press, Kansas City, 1971.

(33) Ibid.

prosperity and/or adversity may come alike to the godly and the ungodly; and

- the book demonstrates what has always been true, that faith in God and piety may and do thrive even in the total absence of temporal prosperity. **"God's people serve him for his own sake, not merely for the temporary reward his service generally brings; they serve him even in overwhelming trial."** (Andrew Fausset).[34]

CAN DIVINE INTEGRITY SURVIVE HUMAN ADVERSITY?

Bildad began his first speech to Job with the sarcastic words: *"How long will you say these things, and the words of your mouth be a great wind? Does God pervert justice? Or does the Almighty pervert the right?"* He then insists that Job and his children must have sinned viciously to have had such dire misfortunes fall upon them; with the corollary, *"If you will seek God and make supplication to the Almighty though your beginning was small, your latter days will be very great."* (8:1-7).

He spoke the truth when he predicted that Job's latter end would be great; but he spoke falsely when he blamed Job for being a great sinner. Even though Bildad called up the authority of generations of earlier teachers, even though he bade Job remember *"what the fathers have found"*, Job knew he was innocent of any really grave transgression. He had done nothing that could warrant such fierce punishment, especially when it was remembered that many who were grossly wicked enjoyed peace and plenty. The facts seemed to belie all justice or mercy in God: *"It is all one; therefore I say, he destroys both the blameless and the wicked!"* (9:22).

Eliphaz raised a horrified protest against this. He demanded of Job: *"Should a wise man answer with windy knowledge, and fill himself with the east wind? . . . But you are doing away with the fear of God, and hindering meditation before God"* (15:2-4). Then he asserted again that

---

(34) A Commentary on the Old and New Testament by Jamieson, Fausset and Brown; *in loc doc.*

"(the) wise men have told, and their fathers have not hidden . . . (that the) wicked man writhes in pain all his days" – therefore, if Job was writhing in pain it simply exposed his wickedness! (vs. 18-20).

Zophar plucked the same refrain. Bluntly and emphatically he declared that only the wicked suffer, while the righteous are surely *"protected and rest in safety"* (11:18); and as for Job, he should *"know that God was exacting of him less than his guilt deserved!"* (vs. 6).

What the friends said was true of God's general providence; but it ignored the particularities of life, and especially the agony wrought within Job by his knowledge that he was essentially righteous – or at least as much as any man could hope to be. To his friends' claim that God had always been known to prosper the righteous and destroy the wicked, he answered, *"Truly I know that it is so!"* (9:1). His next word, though, is *"BUT . . . !"* As though he were saying: "I know that godliness usually does bring happiness; but there are terrible exceptions, and I am one of them!" He acknowledged that the wicked are often judged; but he steadfastly maintained that he was not a sinner (27:6), and that the mystery of God's providence was inexplicable (28:1 ff).

Job accused his friends of falsely describing God's ways, and he urged them to realise that God could not be honoured by a blind refusal to face facts. He is a God of truth and desires that we be truthful, even if honesty poses agonizing dilemmas for faith (13:6-12). He dismissed his friends with the scornful words, *"Oh that you would keep silence and it would show your wisdom! . . . Your maxims are proverbs of ashes, your defences are defences of clay!"* (vs. 5,12). Then, unable to contain himself any longer, Job burst into bitter accusations against God, of injustice, cruelty, indifference (7:20-21; 9:16-17,22; 10:1-2; 13:15 ff; 21:7 ff.; 23:1; etc.)

Through it all Job was challenging his friends to face the facts; and he was demanding God to prove that his integrity was not impugned by the adversities that often struck down the righteous.

The debate ended with the friends sitting in exasperated silence beneath Job's outbursts, and with Job sitting in obstinate silence before the new insights that Elihu brought to the problem. The question was unresolved: Job's afflictions still seemed to cast a shadow on the honour of God.

Then God spoke. And by another paradox the problem was removed!

CHAPTER NINE:
HE STORY OF JOB – (II)

THE VOICE FROM THE WHIRLWIND

> The book of *Job* is a seeming paradox in that it presents
> an unqualified declaration of faith in the existence of an
> all-wise and all-powerful God at the same time that it
> probes with savage honesty the question of divine justice
> in the lives of men . . . The book of *Job* sets up the case
> of a wholly righteous man, who refuses either to
> repudiate God or compromise his claims to innocence,
> while the friends who have come to comfort him preach
> endless variations on the traditional theme of divine
> reward and retribution. The **"comforters"** and their
> arguments are repudiated by God (42:7-8) who, while he
> does not disclose to Job the reason for his sufferings,
> grants him what he most longed for – a revelation of his
> presence and concern. [35]

The extraordinary thing about God's intervention is his complete silence on all of the questions raised. The Lord neither affirms nor denies that he had struck Job down. Job had demanded, *"If it is not he (who destroys), who then is it?"* (9:24). But God firmly ignored the question. Job had asserted that God destroys both the blameless and the wicked. God made no attempt to justify his actions. The friends had categorically asserted that in the providence of God the righteous flourished while the ungodly perished. The Lord refused to confirm or refute the proposition. God knew that Satan was the immediate cause of Job's miseries, but he did not tell Job.

---

(35) Herbert C. Brichto; source unknown.

The contest was between orthodox theology (the conventional and traditional view that God rewards piety with prosperity) and God's failure to act always in harmony with this theology.

The theology itself was not wrong – scripture teaches it in many places – but it was not adequate to explain the whole range of God's dealings with man.

THE DIVINE SOLUTION

Did the Lord then offer Job no solution to his moral dilemma? Did he ignore altogether the patriarch's tears?

Certainly, God did decline to solve the problem by presenting an alternative or more comprehensive theodicy. He refused to enter the debate at that human level. But he did offer his servants something far better: Himself!

In a series of magnificent visions that displayed his wisdom, glory, and power, the Lord reduced the four protagonists to astonished silence.

Even more fascinating is the discovery that all of the wonders Job was bidden to contemplate were related to the natural creation. As J. Sidlow Baxter writes –

> By simply exposing Job's profound ignorance of God's natural government it (revealed) his utter incapacity to pass judgment on that which is far more incomprehensible and mysterious, God's moral government. [36]

And what is the lesson in all this?

> The author's purpose is to portray the folly of mere human wisdom, however great it may be regarded, in contrast to the divine wisdom in the affairs of men. [37]

---

(36) Op. cit., pg. 69.

(37) C.W. Carter; Wesleyan Bible Commentary, Vol. 2; pg. 15; Eerdmans Pub. Co, Grand Rapids; 1973.

It is a striking reminder of the inadequacy of human horizons for a proper understanding of the problem of suffering . . . (it) is an eloquent commentary on the inadequacy of the human mind to reduce the complexity of the problem of suffering to some consistent pattern. It is a book where silent men accomplish more than speaking men – cp. 2:13; 13:5. [38]

The Wise in Israel sought to understand God and his ways by studying the great uniformities of human experience, by reason illuminated by *"the fear of the Lord"*. *Proverbs* is a typical example of their understanding of life. *Job* is a flaming protest, less against the basic concept of *Proverbs* that a God-fearing life brings prosperity (while godlessness brings suffering and destruction), than against the idea that thereby the ways of God are fully grasped. Job is not a type; he is the exception that makes folly of the assumption that through normal experience the depths of God's wisdom and working can be fully appreciated . . . The book does not set out to answer the problem of suffering but to proclaim a God so great that no answer is needed, for it would transcend the finite mind if given. [39]

So we can say with S. R. Driver that the principal aim of the book is negative; it sets out to controvert the still dominant theory that all suffering proceeds from sin, and to show that God's retributive justice is not the only principle by which men are governed.

Elihu, as we shall see, came close to a proper understanding of Job's case; but not even his explanation was openly endorsed by God. Elihu received a kind of negative endorsement by the fact that he was not rebuked (cp. 42:7,9); but the Lord's ultimate answer is to insist that no

---

(38) New Bible Commentary; IVF, London, 1967; pg.388.

(39) New Bible Dictionary, IVF, London, 1967; pg. 637.

man or woman can ever finally understand divine providence. We have
to rest trustfully in two things –

> *For now we see in a mirror dimly, but then face to face.*
> *Now I know in part; then I shall understand fully . . . and*
> *. . . We know that in everything God works for good with*
> *those who love him, who are called according to his*
> *purpose (1 Co 13:12; Ro 8:28).*

SILENCE IS GOLDEN!

The fact is, any attempt to assign a reason for Job's sufferings will run
the speaker into an ethical morass – which has not stopped some brave
souls from trying to be wiser than the Almighty! Those brash adventurers
cleverly find many good reasons for Job's misfortunes!

For example, a booklet was sent to me recently titled *Job: The Truth
Behind The Tragedy*. It's author claims to have located the exact reasons
for Job's plight. He lists them as the patriarch's "fear, unbelief, self-pity,
and self-righteousness."

Let me quote here part of a letter I wrote in reply to that booklet (I have
expanded the original a little) –

> Your booklet seems to me to miss the whole point of the
> story of Job, which is the ultimate mystery of human
> suffering, and the unfairness of life. The tragedy of Job's
> pain remains just that, a tragedy. The Bible makes no
> attempt to explain why such a succession of disasters fell
> upon Job but not upon his friends – yet surely they were
> just as guilty of various spiritual faults as Job was? Nor
> do the scriptures offer any reason for the opposite
> problem: why some who are godly and firm in faith gain
> swift renown and prosperity, while others who are
> equally praiseworthy find that life is a string of
> disappointments.
>
> This letter is not the place for a detailed comment on
> your booklet, but I would suggest you ponder the
> following –

1) You re-write Job 42:11, saying that it uses a "hopal" (Hebrew)

conjugation and should read "God was caused to allow . . . " Then you claim that "by Job's unbelief, fear, and self-righteousness, God was caused to allow those (tragedies) to come on Job. God had no choice; Job brought them on himself and God could not do anything until Job began moving in faith again" (pg. 43,44). That is a tortured use of Hebrew. By any normal reading of the idiom of either the Masoretic or LXX text of Job 42:11, the clause does say plainly, "They comforted Job for all the troubles the Lord had brought upon him." That statement may be embarrassing to a certain group of doctrinaire faith-preachers; but the biblical authors were obviously able to accept it with comfort. Of course, to the ancient Hebrews it would have been astonishing that anyone would be troubled by the statement. Whether or not God did the deed by his own hand, or merely permitted it to be done, he was still seen to be the final cause of every event in life (Is 45:7, plus numerous similar references).

2)   Even if that is still denied, and your reading of Job 42:11 is accepted, it must at least be allowed that God did permit Satan to afflict Job. The question then becomes, "Did God have a reason for giving the devil such permission?" If he did, the Bible is silent about it. When the Lord finally appeared to Job, he answered none of the patriarch's questions; he offered no explanation either of his divine action or inaction; he simple showed Job his glory. It was enough. Job got no answers; but he did abandon his questions!

3)   It is poor theology to suggest that any fault of Job's was the prime cause of his sufferings. Actually, Yahweh himself declared that Satan had incited him to act against Job "without any cause" (2:3). Further, an impossible moral dilemma is created as soon as any attempt is made to go past the basic silence of scripture about the causes of Job's misery. Many, like yourself, have tried to find a reason in Job's "fear" and "self-righteousness", and so on. But multitudes of people (including Job's friends) have been guilty of such sins, and far worse, without anything like Job's troubles coming upon them.

4)   Someone might say that God either caused or allowed Job's pains in order to bring him to repentance and faith. But where does that leave his sons and daughters who were killed? Did their moral development mean nothing to God? And if it is said (very callously) that they deserved their fate, what about the deaths of Job's many servants – some of whom were

killed by the Sabeans, some by the Chaldeans, but the remainder by "the fire of God". How many people do you suppose God is willing to kill or have killed in order to perfect one man? What chance of repentance or reformation did they have? Did they have to die just because Job was self-righteous?

5)   Of course, to ask such foolish questions is to expose the absurdity, if not the blasphemy, of any attempt to find reasons for Job's tragedy – a tragedy that he never ceased to feel, for even after his fortunes had been restored he still needed "consoling" (42:10-11).

6)   Despite what you may think from the above, I do preach faith, I believe in the healing covenant, I teach people to expect success and prosperity within the limits of God's purpose for their lives. But I also recognise that for the present "we see through a dark glass" (1 Co 13:12), and upon many beautiful people miseries do come, the causes of which may remain unknown and unknowable. Sometimes, like Job, their prosperity is restored, but sometimes not. For such people, the answer to the problem of Job (and their own problem) is not in the epilogue (which is finally irrelevant to the body of the drama), but in the patriarch's vision of the glory of God. For whether or not his riches had been given back to him, having seen God, Job was satisfied! (42:1-6)

THE PROBLEM IS ANCIENT

Some one may suggest that Job was a special case, and that his experience cannot be cited as a guide to the way God deals with other people. But I would say in response, "Have you never read the Old Testament, especially the psalms and the prophets?"

There are many places where the servants of God, with tears, complain about the divine behaviour leaving them bewildered and hurt. Philip Yancey tells how Jeremiah grappled with this problem –

> (The prophet) writhed over the seeming powerlessness of God. He put the question to God directly: *"Why are you like a man taken by surprise, like a warrior powerless to save?"* The atheistic philosopher Voltaire could not have put it better: How can an all-powerful and all-loving God permit such a messed-up world?

> To the prophets, it seemed God was pulling farther and
> farther away. Why do godless nations flourish? they
> asked. Why so many natural disasters? Why such
> poverty and depravity in the world? Why so few
> miracles? Where are you God? Why don't you speak to
> us, as you used to? Show yourself, break your silence.
> For God's sake, literally, act! [40]

How can God, having the power to prevent it, watch little children being
tortured, mutilated, starved, broken, and do nothing to prevent it? How
can he sit idly by, while a maiden is brutally raped, her bones broken, her
flesh burned, her throat slit? What would you think of your neighbour, if
he had the power to help you, yet walked on and ignored your cry for
pity?

The OT offers only the solution given in *Job* – a vision of the glory of
God. The NT adds to that the mystery of the cross – how the Father
permitted his only Son to be brutally crucified, yet out of such
unfathomable cruelty endless life has arisen.

Yet still the anguished heart yearns for more light, which it seems we
shall never see this side of the resurrection. As Paul wrote: *"Now we see
but a poor reflection; then we shall see face to face. Now I know in part;
then I shall know fully, even as I am known"* (1 Co 13:12). In that
promise faith must rest.

See *Jeremiah 14:8-9*. A little later, Jeremiah speaks even more bitterly,
actually accusing God of being a liar: *"Why is my pain unending, and my
wound grievous and incurable? Will you be to me like a deceptive brook,
like a spring that fails?"* (15:18). He reckoned the word of God was like
a desert mirage, promising everything but producing nothing. See also
Habakkuk 1:1-4 and *Isaiah 45:15*, along with numerous other verses,

---

(40) From an article in *Christianity Today*, Oct 1987, pg. 18. This problem is
called theodicy = "the vindication of divine justice in the presence of
unrestrained evil." No truly satisfactory solution has ever been presented,
and thoughtful, sensitive people still agonise over the appalling inequities of
life.

plus the many psalms of lament, especially *Psalm 88*, which is unyielding in its bleakness.

Sometimes the Lord responded to those complaints, in one way or another; but just as often heaven was silent, leaving only an unspoken demand for trust (despite any contrary evidence) in the ultimately benevolent purpose of God (cp. He 10:35-39).

SICKNESS AND PROVIDENCE

Perhaps the major paradox in *Job* lies in the rebuke of Eliphaz, Bildad, and Zophar for arguing on behalf of a view that is actually taught in many parts of scripture: that is, the view that piety brings prosperity. The first chapters in this series, and large parts of other *VCC* chapters, are devoted to this same orthodox view! It is taught in *Psalm 37*; it is emphasised in many *Proverbs*; it is part of the teaching of Christ (Mt 6:31-33, and cp. 3 Jn 2). And scores of other verses could be cited.

Those promises are true, and we are right to lay hold of them by faith. Yet Job stands as the anguished representative of all those for whom the promise has not been fulfilled, or for whom its realisation has been delayed. And this is especially true of sickness. It is interesting to note that Job suffered disaster after disaster without complaint until his own body was afflicted, but then he *"opened his mouth and cursed the day of his birth"* (1:20-22; 3:1). Even Satan recognised that this would be so (2:4-5; although Job did not actually curse God, 2:10, at least not vindictively).

Job himself basically believed the orthodox view (9:2); his pain arose from the seeming failure of the promise in his case. The only defence his friends offered was to reiterate their traditional concept. Thus Eliphaz argued that God was chastising Job for wrongdoing, but if Job repented he would again find healing and happiness (5:17-27). Bildad also, insisted that repentance and righteousness would bring laughter once again to Job (8:20-22).

Job had no quarrel with those ideas. He simply maintained that he had already repented, he was already as godly as mortal man could hope to be. If his distress were truly the inescapable dole of his sin, why then were others not equally punished?

Pondering this mystery drove Job to raise three basic issues:

- no man is truly righteous in himself or can ever hope to be (9:2-3); so that no man ever has any valid personal claim on God for his favour; in any case

- God is so powerful he can disdain any adversary, for *"Behold, he snatches away; who can hinder him? Who will say to him, 'What doest thou?'"* (9:12); so that

- whether or not a man is innocent of gross sin he finally has to cast himself upon God's mercy (9:14-15), for neither justice, strength, nor innocence can compel God to act against his own will (9:19-20).

But that brought Job to the heart of the problem: of what use is it to cry out to God when the facts seem to belie all mercy or justice in God? (9:22). None of the friends could offer a satisfactory solution and the debate fell silent.

Then Elihu spoke.

CHAPTER TEN:
THE STORY OF JOB – (III)

THE NEEDED REDEEMER

Being a young man, Elihu had waited patiently while his elders debated (32:4-7); but now they were silent, so he claimed the right to speak. He displayed a high measure of wisdom and insight, claiming indeed that he was speaking by direct inspiration from the Almighty (32:8,18-20; 33:4; although it should be noted that Eliphaz made a similar claim, 4:12-16).

In some ways Elihu's remarks were just as inadequate as the others – he tended still to repeat the orthodox view; he failed to see how special was Job's case; he failed also to see the hand of Satan behind Job's afflictions. But he was more careful in his judgments, and he more nearly approached the truth of the matter. He also spoke more as a friend than as a dogmatist. He was the only one who addressed Job by name (33:1,31; 37:14); and he made an attempt to answer Job's cry for someone who would maintain his right with God, who would act as an umpire between himself and God – but one who would not fill him with dread and terrify him (16:21; 23:3; 9:33; 13:21).

So Elihu offered his services, saying that God had given him this very task, that he would give Job's answer to God, and that Job need have no fear of him, because he too was *"formed from a piece of clay"* (33:1-7).

ELIHU'S SPEECH

A DIFFERENT VIEW

Elihu condensed Job's speeches into two complaints:

- God has capriciously wronged an innocent man (33:8-11); and

- it profits a man nothing to delight in God (34:7-9).

The first complaint is rebutted in *33:12-33* and *34:10-37*; the second, in *35:1-16*.

In the course of these rebuttals Elihu rebuked Job and his friends together. The friends, for their dogmatic assertion that disaster is always linked with divine displeasure; and Job, for his dogmatic assertion of his innocence, even to the extent of accusing God of injustice.

Elihu agrees that affliction may be retributive (34:11; 36:6,11-12); but he insists that our troubles may instead serve a disciplinary and maturing purpose – they do not always prove great sin (as the friends had argued), neither can the sufferer claim to be free of sin (as Job had maintained). Elihu displays a deeper reverence in the presence of God and a deeper awareness of the true nature of sin than the other protagonists.

But Elihu's major contribution was to show that God relates to his servants not merely as Lord or Judge, but more importantly, as Father and Teacher (cp. 35:11; 36:22). Although he cannot reveal to us his ultimately unknowable purposes, God nonetheless expresses his Fatherhood and draws us on to maturity by leading us through the vale of tears. So the young preacher pressed these ideas upon Job:

- *"God opens the ears of men, and terrifies them with warnings, that he may turn man aside from his deed, and cut off pride from a man"* (33:16-17).

- *"Man is chastened with pain upon his bed . . . to bring back his soul from the Pit, that he may see the light of life"* (33:19,29-30).

- in affliction, God desires that we should turn to him and say, *"I have borne chastisement (as a child submits to his father's discipline) I will not offend anymore; teach me what I do not see; if I have done iniquity I will do it no more"* (34:31-32).

- in affliction, God desires that we should cry, *"Where is God my Maker, who gives songs in the night, who teaches us more than the beasts of the earth?"* (35:10-11).

- *"If they are bound in fetters and caught in the cords of affliction . . . he opens their ears to instruction . . . If they hearken and serve him, they complete their days in prosperity, and their years in pleasantness"* (36:8-12).

- *"He delivers the afflicted by their affliction, and opens their ear by adversity"* (36:15).

- *"He also allured you out of distress into a broad place where there was no cramping, and what was set on your table was full of fatness"* (36:16).

- *"Behold, God is exalted in his power; who is a teacher like him? Who has prescribed for him his way, or who can say, 'Thou hast done wrong'?"* (16:22-23).

This thought of God as a Teacher, "intent on steering man through a rough and thorny maze of pain to a deeper experience of himself," is the new concept Elihu brought into the debate. This concept, of course, also figures prominently in the NT (cp. He 12:5-13; 1 Co 11:30-32; 2 Co 4:17; Jn 15:2; Re 3:19; 1 Pe 1:7).

In the course of his argument, Elihu dealt with a number of related themes –

HAS GOD SPOKEN?

Job had voiced against God the accusation, *"He will answer none of my words!"* (33:13). Elihu takes up the challenge, and points out that God does in fact speak to his servants in several different ways. The problem is not that God is not speaking but that men are not listening. If they would pause to hear they would find *"God does speak – now one way, now another – though man may not perceive it . . . God does all these things to a man – twice, even three times"* (33:14,29).

Elihu lists some of the ways God reaches out to his people –

- by *"dreams, in a vision of the night . . . God opens the ears of men"* (33:15-16).

- by an onslaught of wasting sickness God seeks to *"keep back his soul from the Pit, his life from perishing by the sword"* (33:18-22).

- by sending *"an angel, a mediator, one of the thousand, to declare to man what is right for him"* (33:23) – *"angel"* here probably means a human servant of God, whether prophet, priest, pastor, or just a friend wise in the ways of God (like Elihu himself). But whether angel or man, God is not short of such servants, for the expression *"one of the thousand"* is a metaphor expressing the vast number of messengers upon whom God can call. If we are willing to listen, God can always find an *"angel"* to speak for him!

- and God himself added to the list when he went beyond even Elihu's expectations and personally *"answered Job out of the whirlwind!"* (38:1).

For us there is both a similarity and a contrast here. The similarity is, God still speaks to his people today by the same channels he used in Job's day. The contrast is, God speaks more strongly through Christ: *"In many and various ways God spoke of old to our fathers by the prophets; but in these last days he has spoken to us by his Son, whom he appointed the heir of all things through whom also he created the worlds"* (1:1-2). The voice of Jesus, while it has certainly not removed all mystery from life, nonetheless speaks with far greater clarity and authority than any who spoke before. In him the words of Elihu have found a fulfilment that the young teacher could not possibly have imagined.

Look again at Elihu's unconscious prophecy of Christ (33:23-28):

- *"If there be . . . a mediator . . . to declare to man what is right for him."* For us there is but one mediator, who stands interceding between us and God, Jesus Christ the Righteous. He has spoken the only right word, the everlasting gospel.

- *"He is gracious to him, and says, 'Deliver him from going down into the Pit!'"* We rest on the grace of Christ who *"is able for all time to save those who draw near to God through him, since he always lives to make intercession for them"* (He 7:25).

- *"I have found a ransom."* We look at no other than Christ who *"came not to be served, but to serve, and to give his life as a ransom for many"* (Mt 20:28; 1 Ti 2:6).

- and then see the promise that lies in the ransom offered by this Mediator: *"Let his flesh become fresh with youth; let him return to the days of his youthful vigor"* (cp. Jn 10:10; 3 Jn 2; etc.

- in response to this word of life, *"man prays to God, and he accepts him, (and) he comes into (God's) presence with joy. (Then) he recounts to men his salvation, and he sings before men, and says, '(God) has redeemed my soul from going down into the Pit, and my life shall see the light.'"*

GOD CANNOT BE UNJUST

Job had accused God of capriciousness and injustice. Elihu points out the absurdity of such an idea (34:10-20). He demands, *"Shall one who hates justice govern?"* (vs.17). The idea is, will not a mere earthly king who is unjust, arbitrary, capricious, soon bring his realm to ruin? How then can you accuse the King of kings of partiality and neglect (vs. 19)?

Again, the breath of all living creatures is in God's hands (vs. 14-15); but if God were really petulant and indifferent to the welfare of the earth, would he so steadily maintain the flow of life? Surely God's perfect knowledge of all things guarantees his perfect justice – unlike earthly courts, where imperfect understanding often leads to injustice (vs. 21-28).

Do you need more?

Then consider God's absolute integrity, the pure righteousness of his character (36:1-19). But chief of all, consider his awesome power. Can it really be imagined that a God so great would ever find it necessary to stoop to petty tyranny (36:22-37:24)?

So Elihu affirms –

> *Of a truth God will not do wickedly, and the Almighty will not pervert justice . . . The Almighty – we cannot find him; he is great in power and justice, and abundant righteousness he will not violate.*

What response can we have to these things other than reverently to fear God, to trust him, and to be careful not to be wise in our own conceit? (34:12; 37:23-24).

WHEN GOD IS SILENT

Elihu also addressed himself to the times when God is apparently silent, when heaven appears to be giving no answer to the cry of the oppressed. He mentions twice –

> *Yes, he hears the cries of those being oppressed. Yet when he chooses not to speak, who can criticise? . . . The*

oppressed may shriek beneath their wrongs . . . yet none
*of them cry to God, asking, "**Where is God my Maker?**"*
. . . But when anyone does cry out this question to him,
he never replies by instant punishment of the tyrants
(34:28-29; 35:9-12; Living Bible).

But does not God's silence, his failure to act at once, betoken
indifference? injustice? weakness? The preacher answers –

Must God tailor his justice to your demands? Must he
change the order of the universe to suit your whims? . . .
But it is false to say he doesn't see what is going on. He
does bring about justice at last, if you will only wait.
(34:33;35:13-16; Living Bible).

A DIVINE ENDORSEMENT

I have mentioned that some commentators remain unimpressed by either
Elihu or his speech; they think he missed the truth as much as any of the
debaters. But three things appear to provide a divine endorsement of the
young man's speech:

- Elihu concluded his remarks with a stirring description of God's
  majesty displayed in nature (36:26-37:24), which theme was at
  once taken up by the Lord himself, when he spoke out of the
  whirlwind.

- God endorsed Elihu's judgment of Job as a man who had
  "spoken words without knowledge" (cp. 35:16; 38:2).

- no repentance was demanded from Elihu. It would seem that
  while he could not give a complete answer to Job's dilemma,
  Elihu's words reflected a true approach to the problem of pain,
  and they did cast at least some light into the darkness.

But it remains true of us, as it was then (and this is the true message of
Job) that the deepest cry of the human heart can be solved in only one
way – by a personal revelation of God himself.

God has given us that revelation in Christ.

HIGHLIGHTS IN *JOB*

THE UMPIRE (9:32-35)

In that passage the patriarch is "yearning for the God of the mysterious, terrifying beyond to reveal himself in the fabric of understandable human experience." He wanted to see God in human form so that *"the dread of him would no longer terrify me . . . Then I would speak without fear of him."* He cried out for God to send an umpire who might stand *"between us, who might lay his hand upon us both."*

> In this cry for an umpire between God and man we see a prophetic reaching out for 'the one mediator between God and men, the man Christ Jesus' (1 Ti 2:5). There was no finally satisfactory answer to Job short of the incarnation. The passage is strongly forward-looking to Bethlehem. [41]

THE REDEEMER (19:23-27)

It is uncertain just how much Job himself understood the full significance of what he was saying. Some commentators and translators contend that Job does here express a deep and thrilling faith in the resurrection, and in a future recompense. [42] Others find much lesser significance in his words. I would suggest –

1) Job does appear to express some confidence in the resurrection and in life beyond the grave. Notice also, although only ten more children were born to him, the number of his children was still reckoned to have doubled, which may indicate a belief that in some sense they were all still alive. In other words, although the former ten children were dead,

---

(41) New Bible Commentary; pg. 394.

(42) For example, Kenneth Taylor translates the passage thus: *"I know that my Redeemer lives, and that he will stand upon the earth at last. And I know that after this body has decayed, this body shall see God! Then he will be on my side! . . . Yes, I shall see him, not as a stranger, but as a friend! What a glorious hope!"* (Living Bible).

they were not lost. Kenneth Taylor's rendering of 14:13 conveys an inkling of belief in a future resurrection: "Oh, that you would hide me with the dead, and forget me there until your anger ends; but mark your calendar to think of me again!"

2)   However, it seems unreasonable to credit Job with strong faith in the resurrection. His remarkable words in 19:25-26 may well have been prompted by a sudden gleam of divine revelation, but the context in which they are set shows that Job's usual perception of the resurrection was rather dim. For example, he himself, having just expressed some confidence that God will meet him again after death, seems to shrink back from his own boldness, for he immediately asks: "If a man dies, will he live again?" (14:14).

If he could just find a way to answer that question in the affirmative, then, he says, *"All the days of my service I would wait, till my release should come."* But his glimpse of an after-life is soon dissipated, and he lapses again into despair, seeing only a prospect of pitiless death and decay (vs. 18-22).

So it must be admitted that while Job, in brief flashes of insight and faith, alludes to the resurrection, and to the recompense God will give beyond the grave, this concept obviously did not fill his consciousness as it does ours. Andrew Fausset writes –

> The doctrine of a future life in which seeming anomalies
> of the present shall be cleared up would have given the
> main solution to the problem. But as yet this great truth
> was kept less prominent until the appearing of our
> Saviour Jesus Christ who hath abolished death and
> brought life and immortality to light through the gospel!

3)   Therefore, because the patriarchal hope of the resurrection was so shadowy, both Job and the justice of God had to be vindicated by a restoration of Job's material wealth. This is not to say that we Christians dispense with temporal prosperity in order to gain a reward in heaven, nor that Job surrendered his eternal reward because he enjoyed vast riches on earth. Job is as sure of his place in the resurrection and of his share in the glories of heaven as we are. But it does mean, since the Redeemer has come and shown his victory over both life and death, we Christians can be largely indifferent to worldly riches. We may generally

expect our piety to be rewarded by the blessing and favour of God; but our real goal is to obtain the kingdom of God and to lay up treasures in heaven.

E. S. P. Heavenor comments –

> Many have taken strong exception to the portrayal of the material tokens of the divine approval (of Job) . . . (But) at a time when there was no clear picture of a life after death, how could the fact that righteousness is woven into the very texture of reality, and must ultimately bear the stamp of God's vindication, be demonstrated unless on the canvas of the present life? There is no inconsistency in this since the aim of the book has not been to deny that there is a connection between righteousness and material prosperity, but only (to deny) that the connection is invariable. [43]

4)   From our vantage point, then, the words of Job about the Redeemer have a richer meaning than they could have had for him. We can re-phrase his statement: "For I know that my Redeemer lives, and that at last he has stood upon the earth!" From that great fact of history we can affirm with unwavering confidence that "after my skin has been destroyed, then without my flesh I shall see God!" (19:26; RSV margin).

Our faith in Christ's resurrection brings us several sublime benefits:

- as the remainder of these chapters will seek to demonstrate, we gain a reinforced and **"better"** promise of healing, abundant life, and prosperity.

- we enter into a wonderful relationship with the Father as his own dear children.

One of the results of that relationship is that he is at times constrained to *"treat us as sons"* by inflicting discipline on us (He 12:5-13). This

---

(43) New Bible Commentary; pg. 411

discipline may reach to *"the shedding of blood . . . weakness and lameness."*

During the exercise of divine chastening the Lord may or may not reveal his hidden eternal purpose. Our part is to do what we can to secure healing from his hand (cp. He 12:11-13); but when chastening takes the form of persecution, or of the loss of riches, or where death intervenes, then we must submit to the providence of God, trusting that the day of resurrection will requite his justice and secure our glorious inheritance.

BELIEF IN GOD (12:7-25)

To me one of the most impressive aspects of *Job* is this: none of the men in the story ever thought to question the existence of God. That, of course, is a feature of the entire Bible. The glib atheism that guides many people in their handling of the mysteries of life is completely absent from scripture. The biblical characters reveal an intense awareness of God that none of the vicissitudes of life could shake. They might accuse God of unfairness, of injustice, of arbitrary misuse of power (as Job did) but they could never deny God himself.

Concerning the Lord, Job, even in his misery, is compelled to bear witness: *"With God are wisdom and might; he has counsel and understanding. If he tears down, none can rebuild; if he shuts a man in, none can open."* (vs. 13-14)

Faith like that is in the end invincible.

JOB'S HEALING

It needs to be remembered that the main story of Job's life is not one of pain and misery, but rather of prosperity, health, and happiness. True, he carried to his grave the emotional and spiritual scars of the terrible succession of disasters that befell him. But those tragedies were all compressed into the space of a few months (cp. 7:3). He was well advanced in years at the time of his trial (32:6-7), and those years had been richly prosperous under the hand of God (1:1-3). Following his months of trouble, he lived a further 140 years in great peace and contentment (42:12-17).

Despite the afflictions of Satan, and the chastening of the Lord that lay so heavily on him for a while, Job's life is really an example of the marvellous ability of God to heal his people and to bless all their days with health and happiness.

It is *"strange"* and *"unpleasant"* work for a father to punish his child, and so it is with God (Is 28:21; Ez 18:23; 33:11). A father occasionally disciplines his child because he must; the higher purposes of fatherhood demand chastening, both to punish wrongdoing, and to form character. But the true expression of a father's love is found in promoting the health and happiness of his child. The child seeks this from his father, not discipline. So our approach to the Father should be one of confident expectation that he will honour his covenant of healing, and bring us joy and abundance in life.

Yet our wisdom must remain limited. We are but children. So in all things – whether green pastures, still waters, or the valley of death – we must submit ourselves to him. If the promise is not fulfilled to us now, it will be in the resurrection.

There is tension here between a bold appropriation of the promise of God and humble submission to the providence of God. But this tension exists in many parts of the Bible. It will not be overcome by refusing to acknowledge its existence. Rather, our task is to hear the whole message of scripture and then allow the Holy Spirit to apply that part which speaks to our present need.

To conclude: there are mysteries in the outworking of the healing covenant to which I have no answer. Yet the covenant remains. The promise is powerful. In the darkest hour, the call still comes to rise up in faith, to believe God, and to experience his mighty deliverance.

CHAPTER ELEVEN:

DOCTORS IN THE BIBLE

God and the Doctor we alike adore,
But only when in danger, not before;
The danger o'er, both are alike requited,
God is forgotten, and the Doctor slighted!

– John Owen, c. 1600

T o ignore either physician or God is surely foolish. The wise person will avail himself of every gift and skill the Lord has placed among mankind. It is equally irresponsible to focus wholly upon God and forget the physician, or to focus wholly upon the physician and forget God.

Of course, some who have had an unhappy experience with medicine may be inclined to echo the cynicism of Francis Quarles (c. 1640).

> Physicians are, of all men, the most happy. What good success so ever they have, the world proclaimeth; and what faults they commit, the earth covereth.

Or perhaps the unkind cut of Baron von Liebnitz (1646-1716).

> I often say a great doctor kills more people than a great general!

But physicians are only human. They have surely brought comfort and ease to vastly more people than by ignorance they have harmed. And among the company of physicians there have always been many who have aspired to fulfil Plato's model –

> No physician, insofar as he is a physician, considers his own good in what he prescribes, but the good of his patient; for the true physician is also a ruler, having the human body as a subject, and is not a mere money-maker.

> – The Republic I.342.D

But what does the Bible say about doctors?

MEDICINE AND THE COVENANT

Physicians are mentioned in the following places: Genesis 50:2; 2 Chronicles 16:12; Job 13:4; Jeremiah 8:22; Matthew 9:12; Mark 2:17; 5:26; Luke 4:23; 5:31; 8:43; Colossians 4:14.

Medicine is mentioned in Proverbs 17:22; Jeremiah 8:22; 30:13; 46:11; 51:8; Ezekiel 47:12.

Generally speaking, those references are either favourable or neutral; thus

- at least some medicines are classed as **"good"**

- by calling his friends **"worthless"** physicians, Job inferred that there were other **"good"** physicians

- the frequent and familiar references to medicines, healing, and doctors imply that the people often gained benefit from the medical care that was available

- Christ himself implied that the sick should resort to a doctor.

Again, Asa was condemned, not because he turned to the doctors, but because he forgot the Lord. Nor should criticism of the medical fraternity be found in the case of the woman who spent all her money on doctors without improvement – the same can happen today! Then, as now, doctors were sometimes successful, sometimes failed.

The Bible really has very little to say about doctors and medicines – which is not surprising, given the primitive state of medical science in ancient times. Indeed, until quite recent times, John Dryden's advice, given in 1700, was probably the best, except when illness was truly dire–

> Better to hunt in fields, for health unbought,
> Than fee the doctor for a nauseous draught.
> The wise, for cure, on exercise depend;
> God never made his work for man to mend.
> – from a *Letter*

Nonetheless, despite the horrors inflicted upon their terrified patients by many ancient physicians, it is still possible to discern in scripture a general acceptance of physicians and medicines and an endorsement of the benefits they bring mankind.

Certainly the Bible does not criticise those who seek medical help, nor does it forbid the use of medicines. On the contrary, it is surely wisdom to avail ourselves of every natural help or remedy that is offered to us. God is sparing of his miracles, and he does not usually do for us what we can do for ourselves. It is not unbelief to use medicine in a time of illness, but rather recognition of a principle that is openly expressed in both the Bible and life: first that which is natural, then that which is spiritual. The psalmist expresses the ordinary rule of scripture –

> (All things) look to thee, to give them their food in due season. When thou givest to them, they gather it up (*Ps 104:27-28*).

God gives, but we must gather. We should not expect the Lord to gather what we are able to gather for ourselves. Hence the general approval of God must rest upon the labours of all those who have gathered knowledge and skill in healing and who seek to relieve the distress of those who are sick. Surely this alone is logical: only when you truly believe it is the will of God for you to be made well can you honestly accept medical treatment! If healing is the will of God, then those who labour to make the sick well are pursuing a divine goal. But a person who believes disease is the will of God violates his own conviction when he strives to get well. If God wants you to be sick then you should meekly resign yourself to your disease and have nothing to do with pills, potions, or physicians!

The Bible references to medicines and physicians are rather meagre; but there is a fascinating passage in that remarkable apocryphal book, Ecclesiasticus. [44] Opinions will differ as to how much inspiration or

---

(44) <u>Ecclesiasticus</u> (or, <u>The Wisdom of Sirach</u>) was written by Joshua ben Sirach c. 180 BC It belongs among the Wisdom writings of Israel, and is focused on advice for successful living. Its maxims, warnings, instructions, embrace almost every area of human experience. It was held in high honour by the Jews, and was immensely popular among the early Christians. It is quoted from, or alluded to, some 30 times in the NT, and was treated as scripture by many of the Church Fathers. It is included in

. . . continued on next page.

authority should be accorded Ecclesiasticus; but at the very least it may be said to reflect the wisdom, insight, and experience of one of the greatest of the old Jewish teachers. On the question of physicians Joshua ben Sirach wrote –

> Honour the doctor for his services,
>> for the Lord created him.
> His skill comes from the Most High,
>> and he is rewarded by kings.
> The doctor's knowledge gives him high standing
>> and wins him the admiration of the great.
> The Lord has created medicines from the earth,
>> and a sensible man will not disparage them.
> Was it not a tree that sweetened water
>> and so disclosed its properties?
> The Lord has imparted knowledge to men
>> that by their use of his marvels he may win praise;
> By using them the doctor relieves pain,
>> and from them the pharmacist makes up his mixture.
> There is no end to the works of the Lord,
>> who spreads health over the whole world.
> My son, if you have an illness, do not neglect it,
>> but pray to the Lord, and he will heal you.
> Renounce your faults, amend your ways,
>> and cleanse your heart from all sin.
> Bring a savory offering and bring flour for a token,
>> and pour oil on the sacrifice; be as generous as you can.
> Then call in the doctor, for the Lord created him;
>> do not let him leave you, for you need him.
> There may come a time when your recovery is in their hands;
>> then they too will pray to the Lord
>> to give them success in relieving pain
>> and finding a cure to save their patient's life.
> When a man has sinned against his Maker,

. . . continued from previous page.

Roman Catholic Bibles, but is not accepted as scripture by most Protestants. It should not be confused with the canonical *Ecclesiastes*.

let him put himself in the doctor's hands.
– Sir 38:1-15; New English Bible

MISCELLANEOUS REFERENCES

The remainder of this chapter contains a collection of miscellaneous references to the infliction and healing of disease, drawn from Psalms, Proverbs, the Prophets, and elsewhere. The list is as exhaustive as time has permitted me to make it. But no doubt some references have been omitted. If you discover other passages that should be added to this collection (apart from references which I have quoted in the preceding chapters) please write and tell me.

STATEMENTS THAT SICKNESS ARISES FROM SIN

1)   Loss of appetite, fatal disease, various afflictions, may be a direct consequence of sin – Psalm 107:17-18.

2)   Proverbs 26:2. This proverb has the general sense, "a curse uttered without a proper cause offers you no more threat than a flitting sparrow; it is more likely that a swallow will land on your head than that an unjust curse will find its mark in you." Its intention was probably to rid the people of their superstitious dread of a spoken curse. They were to understand that no curse had any power merely because it was spoken; it had power only if its intended victim gave cause for it to have power.

Over the righteous, those who are protected by God, no curse has any power.

However, on a deeper level, the same principle applies to the curse spoken by God – *Deuteronomy 28:15* ff. This curse is seeking a victim upon whom it may fall, but it can fall only on those who provide cause for it to do so; all others may claim, if not full immunity from the curse, at least the right to be delivered from it if it comes.

The Deuteronomic curse includes, of course, sickness. Does that mean whenever I become ill I must have given God cause to punish me, that he is inflicting upon me the curse of his broken law? It may mean just that, and I should certainly examine myself, and ask God, to see whether it is so (1 Co 11:28-32).

However, sickness is not necessarily an act of punishment; it may arise from a number of factors, such as: the sheer malice of Satan; failure to provide proper care and nourishment of the body; contact with infection; the corruption of death that is in us all; environmental stress; and so on.

But the fact is, there is always some cause underlying the onset of disease, and on many occasions we may need to isolate that cause, and take steps to remove it, before we can be in a position to claim healing from God.

3)   The same theme is repeated by the prophets –

> *The Lord said to me . . . I will not hear their cry by famine, and by pestilence . . . I myself will fight against you with outstretched hand and strong arm, in anger and in fury, and in great wrath. And I will smite the inhabitants of this city, both man and beast; they shall die of a great pestilence . . . Why will you and your people die by the sword, by famine, and by pestilence, as the Lord has spoken? (Je 14:11-12; 21:6; 27:13).*

> *Therefore I have begun to make you sick, to smite you, making you desolate because of your sins (Mi 6:13).*

EXAMPLES OF SICKNESS ARISING FROM SIN

1)   The people of Ashdod were stricken with tumors (1 Sa 5:6).

2)   The people of Bethshemesh were stricken down because they looked into the ark of the Lord (1 Sa 6:19).

3)   Uzzah was slain because he touched the ark (2 Sa 6:6-7).

4)   Because David murdered Uriah, and took his wife Bathsheba, David's son by Bathsheba became very sick and died (2 Sa 12:14-23).

5)   Seventy thousand people died in a terrible plague caused by an illegal numbering of Israel and failure to collect the appointed ransom (2 Sa 24:1-25; Ex 30:11-16). It is noteworthy also that Satan was the prime instigator of this tragic event (1 Ch 21:1), and that the plague was stopped as soon as David offered sacrifice. Once again we see healing being found in a God-appointed atonement.

6) Abijah, the son of king Jereboam, fell sick and died as a direct judgment upon the king's sin (1 Kg 14:1-18). This case is unusual, in that the Lord took the lad, not only in judgment on Jereboam, but also in mercy to the boy, to save him from the brutality and violent death that was to fall on every other male member of the family (vs. 13).

7) Ahaziah, king of Israel, became sick, and might have recovered had he not inquired at the shrine of an idol. But because of his failure to seek healing from the Lord, he died (2 Kg 1:1-4,17).

8) For his idolatry, and wickedness Jereboam was struck down by a stroke, and died (2 Ch 13:20).

9) Jehoram, king of Judah, was warned by a prophet that a dreadful scourge would strike if he did not turn from his iniquity: however he gave no heed to the word of the Lord and died as the prophet had said, in awful suffering (2 Ch 21:12-20).

10) Joash slew one of the Lord's priests (2 Ch 24:20); and as a result he was stricken with great diseases and was finally murdered by his own servants (vs. 25).

11) Uzziah was stricken with leprosy because he violated the law of the Lord (2 Ch 26:16-23). His case is doubly tragic because the early part of his life was marked by a zeal for righteousness, and he was greatly prospered by the Lord (vs. 4-5,15). Once again we are plainly shown that adherence to the word of the Lord can bring health and prosperity, but that ignorance of it, or unbelief in it, or violation of it, may bring disaster.

12) Proud and haughty Nebuchadnezzar was swiftly cast down by the Lord, and left insane until he learned to repent and give glory to God (Da 4:1-37).

13) See the description Amos gives of the terrible desolations that fell on Israel because of their constant sin (Am 4:6-10).

No doubt for all those reasons, and for others like them, Sirach urged his readers to prepare themselves spiritually before the onset of disease – both so that they could escape sickness, or failing that, be able to gain a miracle of answered prayer. The foundation for divine healing should be laid while one is still well, for it may be too late to seek a place of faith once disease has fastened upon the sufferer –

Joshua before you open your mouth, do you not first make sure you know what to say? So too, before sickness strikes you, give attention to your health. . . . Before you fall ill, humble yourself, and if you do sin, hasten to repent. Let nothing stop you from praying, and do not wait for the onset of death before you seek God's mercy. Keep yourself always ready for prayer, and do not be one of those who try the patience of the Almighty. . . . The time to prepare for famine is while you are enjoying plenty; the time to guard against poverty is while you have riches. Between sunrise and sunset everything can change! Things happen quickly when God speaks! So those who are wise will be constantly on guard. Sirach (18:19-27)

BIBLICAL TESTIMONIES OF DIVINE HEALING

The following references indicate the implicit faith many of the saints in Israel had in the healing covenant. The list could probably be extended, but enough is given to show that this faith was not sporadic, but universal among the true people of God. They understood that God had made a definite promise of healing to Israel, and they were bold to claim the fulfilling of that promise. The list is given in scriptural order, and references which seem to me to be especially striking I have underlined.

- ***Joshua 21:45; 23:14***. The promise of God to Israel as given to Moses, definitely included healing. Here Joshua testifies, at the end of his life, that this promise had not once failed.

- ***1 Kings 3:14***. A long life is promised in answer to obedience and faith (cp. 1 Kg 8:37-39,56).

- ***2 Chronicles 6:26-30; 7:11-14***. The latter passage conveys a revelation of the basic reason why God allows suffering – because without it man would soar in arrogance and utterly cut himself off from God. Further, in both of these passages Solomon recognises that an upsurge of disease in the land could come only because of sin, [45] and in his prayer he demonstrates his faith in the covenant promise of God and plainly declares his certainty that God both could and would heal the people (2 Ch 20:9).

- *__Psalm 1:3; 6:1-9__*. David was sick and prayed that God would heal him. He could not accept it was God's will for him to die. He felt his affliction was dishonouring to the Lord, that only his recovery would bring praise to God.

- *__Psalm 18:2,4-6,19; 21:1-4; 22:24; 23:6; 25:16-18; 30:1-3; 31:19-24__*. When sickness and trouble came, David thought the Lord had forsaken him and he rashly declared that the promise of God had failed (vs. 22), but he soon re-gathered his faith, called upon God, and was delivered.

- *__Psalm 32:7-10; 34:4,6-10,12,17-19; 37:3-5,25,39; 38:3-7,21-22; 41:8-10; 42:11; 67:1-2; 70:5; 91:1-16__*. This whole Psalm is a tremendous testimony to the ability of God to deliver his people from every pestilence and every onslaught of Satan. The conditions for its fulfilment are simple:

- that we enter the covenant of the Lord and abide in him (vs. 1)

- that we have a positive, spoken affirmation of trust in God's healing power (vs. 2)

- that we do not allow our love for God to grow cold (vs. 14)

- that we know the authority and might of his name (vs. 14)

- that we are quick to call upon him and claim his promise in the hour of need (vs. 15).

- *__Psalm 102:1-5,17-20; 103:1-5__*, forgiveness of sin and healing of sickness are the two chief benefits of God's covenant. Ps 107:1-

---

(45) Remember though that "sin" may involve not only violation of the moral laws of God, but also of his natural laws of proper hygiene, diet, and so on.

2,6,13-14,20-21,43; 109:21-27; 119:153-156,170; 144:11-15; 145:17-19.

- *Proverbs 3:2,8,22; 4:10,22; 9:10-11; 10:11,16,25; 10:27-30; 11:18-21,30-31; 12:18,21,28; 14:26-27,30; 16:24; 17:22; 18:21; 19:23; 21:21; 22:4; 28:10,18.*

- *Isaiah 33:22,24; 35:4-6,10; 40:29-31; 53:4-5 (cp. Mt 8:14-17); 57:119-21; 58:5-7.*

- *Je 7:23; 8:21-22; 17:14* (pardon and healing coupled together as the word of God); *33:6.*

- ***Ezekiel 34:1-4***. What a scathing criticism the prophet gives of the priests and pastors of Israel who had forgotten the healing covenant and no longer brought deliverance to the people (Ez 47:8-9,12; Da 6:27; Ma 4:2).

Once God has made a promise, that promise is never retracted nor altered. The outward terms or conditions may be changed, but the promise itself, once uttered, becomes immutable (He 6:17-18).

That principle applies to the promise of healing: having once revealed himself as Jehovah-Rapha, *"The-Lord-our-Healer"*, God is eternally bound to be the Physician of his people. He was Great Physician to Israel, he is Great Physician to his church. The promise of healing is ever the same, only the external circumstances of the covenant have altered. In place of the laws and sacrifices of the old dispensation we have now the one sacrifice, Calvary, and the one law, the Gospel of Christ. In fact, far from gaining lesser benefits from the new covenant, the promises of the old have been immeasurably enlarged. The key-note of the new dispensation is "better" (He 7:19,22; 8:6; 9:23; 11:40; 12:24; etc). The Lord Jesus Christ is *"the mediator of a better covenant, established upon better promises."*

The old covenant included a wonderful promise of healing and health. The new covenant contains a better promise than this. In what way is it better? Some people would have us believe that God has "improved" the old promise by changing his mind: now, they say, it is no longer God's will to heal us, rather, he just gives us strength to endure sickness patiently until medicine or surgery effects a kill or cure! Surely that is an evasion of the promise rather than an exposition of it!

This better covenant of today unquestionably includes the same promise of healing as the old: it is better simply because it is now extended freely to all men. It is no longer restricted to Israel, it no longer requires the offering of a sacrifice on a temple altar.

Many scriptures categorically state that the Lord God is immutable both in himself and in his promise. He never changes. What he was, he is! If this is so, then the following references describe God as he is, not merely as he was, and the promises they contain are as valid for us as they were for Israel.

- ***Numbers 23:19-20; Psalm 33:11***. *"The thought of God's heart"* toward Israel of old was one of compassion, pardon, mercy, deliverance, healing; his desire is the same toward our present generation.

- ***Psalm 102:27; Malachi 3:6; Acts 10:34; Hebrews 6:17-18; 13:8***. Each of those references indicates the **"immutability"** of God – that is, while he can change his methods and procedures, God cannot change his basic character or nature. If healing the sick can be shown to be only a part of God's temporary method, then perhaps healing is not for today. However, if those references (and many others quoted throughout these pages) show, as I believe they do, that it is part of God's eternal nature to heal that which is sick, then, divine healing must be for today as much as it was yesterday.

CHAPTER TWELVE:

THE WOUNDED MESSIAH

Text: _Isaiah 53._

> It is really marvellous that Isaiah had so much light, that
> he could depict the mysteries of Christ so clearly and
> fittingly, in fact, more fittingly than even the evangelists,
> with the one exception of Paul, the chosen instrument.
> Otherwise, all scripture scarcely has a passage equal to
> this 53rd chapter of _Isaiah._ [46]

I ndeed, the most profound depiction of the healing covenant in the _Old
Testament_ is found in Isaiah's passionate oracle about the Wounded
Messiah, in which he describes the Saviour as being

MARRED BY GOD

> _His appearance was marred beyond human semblance,
> and his form no longer appeared human (52:14)._

What can those dark expressions mean? How could the Messiah have
lost _"human semblance"_? How could he _"no longer appear human"_?
These are puzzling expressions, and they leave us wondering what
connection they have with our redemption. Was Jesus _really_ so _"marred"_
at Calvary? Just exactly _what_ did Isaiah see in his vision?

Some idea of what the prophet may mean can be gained from the 4^{th-}
century historian Eusebius, who told the story of the early Christian
martyrs –

> A young man by the name of Sanctus, who was a deacon
> in the church at Vienne, also endured marvellously and
> superhumanly all the outrages that he suffered. The

---

(46) Edward M. Plass, op. cit., selection #3668.

wicked men hoped, by the continuance and severity of his tortures, to wring from him something that he ought not to say. But Sanctus girded himself against them with such firmness that they could not force him to tell them even his name, nor what nation or city he came from, nor whether he was a slave or a free man. To all their questions he answered in the Roman tongue only with the words: "I am a Christian.". . . There arose therefore on the part of the governor and the torturers a great desire to conquer Sanctus; but having exhausted all their cruelty, and finding nothing more they could do to him, they finally fastened red hot brass plates to his body. Then his body became a plain witness to his sufferings, being turned into <u>one complete wound and bruise, drawn out of shape, and altogether unlike a human form</u>. [47]

Here was a violence of suffering so terrible that it twisted the young man so much out of shape that he no longer looked human. Similarly –

a young man, whose name was Apphianus, managed to elude the imperial bodyguard, and rushed up to the governor as he was offering a libation to the gods of Rome. Apphianus seized the governor's hand, and loudly urged him to stop calling upon dead gods and to worship instead the living God. When the governor and those who were with him realised what Apphianus was saying, they fell upon him as if they were wild animals, and began to beat and tear at him. After he had manfully endured countless blows over his entire body, they carried him off and threw him into prison. There the torturer confined him in the stocks and stretched his legs for a night and a day. However, though they strove to force him to surrender, he exhibited great constancy under suffering, and remained steadfast through the most terrible torments. His sides were torn with iron hooks,

(47) Paraphrased from Eusebius (circa 264-340), <u>Ecclesiastical History</u> 5.1.20.

not once or twice, but many times, until his very bones and bowels were exposed, and he received so many blows to face and neck, that <u>even his close friends were no longer able to recognise his swollen features</u>. *(Eusebius then describes the even more awful pains that Apphianus was forced to endure, through all of which he remained undaunted in courage and faith. Eventually, nearly dead, but undefeated, he was thrown by his frustrated persecutors over a cliff, into the sea, and drowned.)* [48]

Thus Apphianus too emulated his Master in being so foully beaten that he lost his true *"semblance"*, and was no longer recognisable as the man he had been. Then there was

Sherbil, a pagan priest, who was converted to Christ, and martyred under Trajan, c. 110. Because of his high pagan office, the Roman governor of Edessa determined to make an example of him. So he was first scourged, then hung up and torn with hooks, then strapped into a ball and beaten. But through it all he refused to recant. Then he was stretched until his bones were dislocated, and burnt with hot irons over his entire body. Still remaining firm, many other cruelties were inflicted upon him. More dead than alive he was fixed to an iron frame and scourged *"until there remained not a sound place on him"*, whereupon the judge said: *"Well have I called thee a dead man, because thy feet are burnt and thou carest not, and thy face is scorched and thou holdest thy peace, and nails are driven in between thine eyes and thou takest no account of it, and thy ribs are seen between the furrows torn open by the combs . . . and thy whole body is mangled and maimed with stripes . . .*

(48) Paraphrased from Eusebius, "The Martyrs of Palestine", ch. 4.

Likewise, Habib, an early 4th century deacon, also from Edessa, was scourged by 5 men, who were commanded by the judge –

> "Let him be stretched out and scourged with whips, until there remains not a place in his body upon which he has not been scourged." He suffered also many other fearful manglings, and was finally burnt to death. [49]

In each of those accounts, and in others like them, there are echoes of the oracle of Isaiah. They show what the prophet saw – the Messiah so savagely flogged and mutilated and his body so torn, that it no longer held a human shape. He was marred until his dearest friends could see no resemblance to their familiar companion, beaten until no part of his body remained unmarked.

Thus he suffered. But he was not defeated –

> *See, my Servant will flourish, he will be highly honoured,*
> *he will be exalted to the highest place! (52:13)*

His torment was not in vain, for he suffered not for himself but for us. Therefore the Father raised him to the loftiest splendour. He has gone before us into the heavenlies, there to prepare the way for us one day to join him in his glory. How splendid will that glory be? The measure of *his* suffering is the measure of *our* destiny. He was cast down to the lowest so that we might be raised to the highest. His pain is the forecast of our prosperity, his reduction the guarantee of our riches, his hurt the surety of our healing.

But then Isaiah adds another word to his description of the passion of the Messiah. The prophet describes him as the Man who was

WOUNDED BY GOD

According to a standard Nurses' Dictionary, there are only five kinds of wound, all of which were suffered by Christ (Is 53:5a) –

---

(49) The Ante-Nicene Fathers Vol. Eight, pg. 676 ff, 690 ff.

- ***Contusion***: a blow from a blunt instrument, such as the rods used against him in the palace of the high priest, and by the soldiers in the praetorium (cp. Mi 5:1).

- ***Laceration***: by a tearing instrument, such as a scourge or scraper (Ps 129:3; Is 50:6)

- ***Penetration***: a deep wound or puncture by a pointed instrument, such as the crown of thorns. [50]

- ***Perforation***: piercing right through (Ps 22:16); and note that since crucifixion was introduced into Palestine only after the Roman occupation, such predictions must have been puzzling to the prophets.

- ***Incision***: cut by a sharp instrument (Jn 19:34).

So with great confidence the prophet declared: *"this chastisement that was upon him has made us whole!"* Jesus bore all manner of wounding so that we might find all manner of healing! Nor can this be restricted merely to spiritual healing, that is, inner healing of the spirit alone. Jesus himself went about curing *physical disease* on the strength of this very oracle (Mt 8:14-17). He had no doubt that the promise of God included a remedy for earthly ills, as well as those that belong to the soul.

Further, note how confident he was that the scriptures would infallibly find their fulfilment in him! So confident that he pre-empted the promise, and before he had actually suffered found grace to bring healing to the sick. Why should we suppose that his purpose is any different today? How much more effective must the promise be now that he has indeed fulfilled all its terms on our behalf?

Then the prophet tells us, not only was he marred and wounded for us, but he was also

(50) Although the authenticity of the *Shroud of Turin* is highly suspect, it is nonetheless interesting to note that it shows a full cap of thorns, not just a circlet, and was therefore truly a "crown", which his enemies meant for his disgrace, but has instead become a coronet of glory.

SCARRED BY GOD

Note the strange expression, *"By his <u>stripe</u> we are healed."*

The word in Hebrew is singular, not plural. It is "stripe", which is not the word for the raw wound left by a scourging, but rather for the mark or scar left after a wound has healed (cp. Sir 28:17, "A blow from a whip leaves a scar.")

Is this important? It would seem so, for when Peter wrote his letter, and quoted Isaiah, he used an exact Greek equivalent for the Hebrew word. That is, he too used the word for a "scar" (not a raw wound), and he copied also the singular form used by Isaiah (1 Pe 2:24). The apostle made only one change. Whereas Isaiah used the present tense ("By his scar we <u>are</u> healed"), Peter chose the past tense ("By his scar we <u>were</u> healed"). The reason of course is that the prophet was looking ahead in faith to a work that was not yet done, whereas the apostle could look back on a redemption that is now fully accomplished.

What can we learn from this "scarring" of Christ? It shows –

THE CERTAINTY OF THE ATONEMENT

This scarring, which he alone bears among all the host of heaven, marks him as the Saviour appointed by God. We may at once say three things about this scar –

- *it is a mark of punishment suffered –*

There are several sad references in the Bible to people being flogged as punishment for some fault. Those were savage and brutal times, [51] in which the lash often left its terrible imprint upon human flesh – "A slave who is constantly whipped will never be free of scars." (Sir 23:10).

Similarly, if one asks, Christ can tell the meaning of his scar –

---

(51) See Deuteronomy 25:2-3; Proverbs 10:13; 17:10; 18:6; 19:29; 20:30; 26:3; etc.

"What are these scars upon your body?" He will answer, "They are scars I got in the house of my friends!" (Zc 13:6).

Those who should have been his friends punished him for crimes he did not commit! Then also,

- *it is a mark of status gained –*

Think about how the scars left by the cat-o'-nine-tails showed the toughness of an 18th-century seaman. By a kind of perverse psychology, those old sailors were prone to boast about their hideous floggings, and to reckon that since they had survived the cat's claw no other terrors of the sea could frighten them. Likewise, a sabre slash upon the cheek of a Prussian nobleman was once thought to proved his manhood and courage. It showed also that he was fit to be numbered among the reigning elite. Or again, among the Maoris in New Zealand, nobility was displayed by having one's face tattooed with a fine bamboo chisel and a small hammer. No man could hope to be chief if he could not endure the many agonising hours needed to create a fully carved face.

All those people, and others like them, depended upon some sort of scar to establish their prestige, or to qualify them for office. In the same manner, the Man Isaiah saw in his vision bears in his own body the sign that he is qualified to heal his people (cp. also Is 53:5-6 with Ex 21:5-6.) With the eye of faith, we too may see those marks upon the Saviour, and boldly pronounce him our Great Physician!

A modern physician goes to school, earns a degree, hangs up a brass shingle, and thus proclaims to all that he is qualified to heal. But this Man needs no proof of his skill save the ineradicable testimony of his scar. It marks him forever as the Saviour appointed by the Father for the healing of the nations. It speaks plainly to all who believe that his own blood has sealed for us a covenant of redemption from every ill inflicted by Satan.

- *it is proof of his <u>right</u> to heal –*

No other in heaven carries the mark, and he will carry it for ever (Re 5:6). It is an unquenchable witness to all who query his title of Physician, or who doubt that the price has truly been paid. It is a better mark of his right to heal than that ever gained by any other physician throughout the years of time or across eternity.

THE TOTALITY OF THE ATONEMENT

There is a peculiarity in our text, which I have already mentioned. Although most English translations choose the plural form of the Hebrew and Greek words for "scar", both Isaiah and Peter use the singular form (*"scar"* not *"scars"*). Why? It seems to be a graphic way of showing the horrible severity of the sufferings of Christ (cp. Is 52:14).

Like the young man Sanctus, it could be said of Jesus too that "his body became a plain witness to his sufferings, being turned into <u>one complete wound and bruise, drawn out of shape, and altogether unlike a human form</u>." That is, his wounds were so many that they merged into each other, and could no longer be counted apart, but seemed to be one continuous wound over his entire form. Thus, as the prophet saw in his vision, and as the apostle (who had watched him die) attested, he bears not many "scars", but just the one "scar".

Why did God permit such a horror of mutilation to be committed against his own Son? See again *Isaiah 53:4,10,12*, which says, that just as he carried away our sins, so he also had to *"bear our sicknesses and carry away our pains"*. For us it means that whatever part of our frame sins or gets sick, that same part of Christ was scarred, thus demonstrating that in him God has provided for us total healing for our entire body, soul, and spirit. No wonder the Evangelist was able to write that

> *Jesus journeyed throughout Galilee, teaching in the synagogues, preaching everywhere the good news of the kingdom, and healing <u>every kind</u> of sickness and disease among the people (Mt 4:23).*

Has he changed? Is he no longer moved with compassion? Can it be said reasonably that he lacks either the power or the will to continue healing the sick in our time? How can we continue to trust the promise of pardon (Is 53:5a) if we may no longer trust the promise of healing? (Is 53:5b). Surely they both stand or fall together?

THE FINALITY OF THE ATONEMENT

A scar is a sign of a wound that has healed; it has finality; it shows there will be no further suffering. Thus we can learn from the scar of Christ that complete atonement has been made for our sins, never to be repeated. If the matter is ever questioned, whether in heaven, on earth, or in hell, his scar will for ever speak on behalf of us sinners.

In sickness, a scar marks a disease that has been defeated. Thus an appendectomy scar asserts that whatever else you may eventually die of, it will not be appendicitis! Likewise, if you can believe it, the scar Christ bears conveys a witness of victory over *every* disease that might ever afflict you! In the hour of sickness, let that scar speak to you, declaring its message of disease, all disease, met and overcome. And then raise with your own lips an echo of the prophet's bold affirmation, *"By his scar I am healed!"*

But then comes the most sombre and mysterious part of Isaiah's vision of the wounded Messiah. He declares that Jesus was

DISEASED BY GOD

"It was the will of God to make him sick" (vs. 10, lit.)

Why did God do this terrible thing? Because Jesus had to carry away all our diseases (vs. 4). Compare the word *"bear"* with the same word in verse 12. That is, just as he bore away our *sin* as our surrogate sacrifice, so he bore away our *sickness* as our surrogate sufferer. Note also: he bore our sins, not merely to secure for us pardon but also *victory*; likewise, he bore our diseases, not just to offer consolation but complete *healing.*

If then it was the will of God to make *him* sick, it is surely the will of God to make *us* well! How could anyone doubt this? What could be more certain? Why else would the Father strike down his only Son except to make it possible for us to be raised up?

Jesus in fact may have been the only person in history made sick by the direct action of God. Perhaps in every other case of disease God has used or allowed only second causes, such as Satan, or nature. But in the Messiah's case, no other intervention could be permitted. This dread work had to be done by the Father's own hand, so that the Father's purpose of healing might be infallibly accomplished.

When was Jesus *"made sick"* by God? It was at the cross. I do not mean that he actually became diseased, but that at Calvary all sickness found its consummation in his death. The language used in the oracle must be at least to some degree metaphorical. But the message remains sure. Christ suffered so that we might be saved; he was made sick so that we might be healed.

CONCLUSION

We do not always see Christ as a scarred Surrogate, nor would we wish to do so. In the eye of a Christian, Jesus may display many different aspects, sometimes full of full of grace and beauty, sometimes blazing with splendour and majesty, or perhaps glowing with gentleness and love (cp. Ps 23:1; Re 1:12-16; etc). But in times of sickness – whether of soul or body – we *do* need to see him as the Scarred One. It is then, when we need healing, we should look heavenward and focus our gaze upon the Lamb. Look until you see that he still bears the mark of death upon him (Re 5:6-10) – the death he suffered for our recovery.

Isaiah gives us a description of this process. He shows that when disease has struck us down we need the same kind of spiritual revelation, the same kind of faith-growth, that came to those who first witnessed the Messiah's suffering –

- they began by *"esteeming him smitten by God and afflicted"*

- then, reckoning Christ to be accursed by God, *"they hid their faces from him and despised him"*

- but then they discovered that he was in fact *"wounded for our transgressions, and bruised for our iniquities . . . and <u>by his scar we are healed!</u>"*

Let that same dawning light awaken in your own soul, until you too can say with absolute assurance (echoing both Isaiah and Peter), *"By his scar I am healed!"*

We have already seen how Jesus healed the sick on the basis of his own faith in Isaiah's prophecy. Surely that same faith in the promise of God can release to us today the same healing virtue of Christ.

ADDENDUM:

FAITH AND HEALING

CHAPTER THIRTEEN:

AWAKE! AWAKE!

I saiah, in a vision, saw Judea conquered by the Babylonians. The people were crushed and enslaved, and they called piteously upon the Lord to deliver them, crying, "Awake! Awake!" (Is 51:9). But God turned their prayer back upon them – "Awake! Awake!" said he to the despairing people (52:1-3).

God tells Israel to do for themselves the very thing they were begging him to do for them!

Was he mocking them? No. He was simply saying that since sleepy unbelief had brought them into bondage; only awakening faith could bring them out of it! The prophet told Israel what kind of faith they needed –

SHAKE OFF YOUR DUST

"Awake and shake off your dust!"

We have to confront the fact that our greatest enemy is never anything outside of us, but it is *always* within our own spirits. It consists of a spiritual lethargy that often engulfs us, a lifeless passivity, that deathly dullness that enervates both mind and soul. Inevitably, we lapse into quiescent and helpless despair. Our spirits become dull and emaciated. Faith and vigour vanish from them as the mist evaporates before the rising sun.

Coupled with this decay of faith is a spiritual blindness. We become engrossed in our own darkness and we lose sight of the glory of God that is all around us. He never leaves us without sight of his power and majesty, [52] yet it seems to us, in our spiritual slumber, that it is actually

---

(52) Romans 1:19-20; Psalm 19:1-4.

God who is asleep. So, like Israel, we cry out, *"Awake, O Lord!"* But he was never asleep! [53] The awakening needs to take place, not in heaven, but in our own faith.

Then, when the devil finds the people of God so asleep, he gets them sitting in the dust like those ancient mourning Israelites. There they crouched, clothed in rags, scooping up handfuls of dust and sprinkling it over their heads, wailing, moaning, groaning, and complaining. That's no place for a man or a woman of faith to be!

The Father's response was inevitable: *"Wake up and shake off that dust!"*

God is still on the throne. He is still in control. The door is open to the miracle you need. God has not closed it and the devil can't.

PUT ON YOUR STRENGTH

In the Assyrian room of the British Museum there is a wall inscription that was taken from the palace of the great monarch Sennacherib. It shows a long line of wretched men and women whom Sennacherib had enslaved as he marched across the Middle East, spreading the Assyrian terror far and wide. The captives are yoked together at the neck, with chains hanging from one to the other. They are naked – a typical Assyrian tactic to humiliate and break the spirit of a slave – and their arms are manacled behind them.

Isaiah caught that very scene in his vision. He heard the despairing cry of the people, battering heaven with their plea, *"Awake! Awake!"* He saw them groaning under their chains and the slave-driver's lash.

Yet the prophet then turned to those same helpless captives and sternly commanded, *"Put on your strength and shake the chains off your neck!"*

Was this some hideous mockery? Did he lack all heart? Was he blind to their helplessness?

(53) Psalm 121:4-5.

It was none of those things. Rather, it was a demand that they begin to change something inside their own spirits. He was saying that their chains had only as much strength as they allowed them to have, that their bonds were only as real as they reckoned them to be. They had but to cast off their fears, throw away their despair, and renew their confidence in God. They would soon find their iron chains turning into straw ropes that could be broken by the snap of a finger.

Once when I was a child I visited a circus and noticed something strange: the great elephants that led the circus parade were tethered by a slender cord to a small wooden stake. I wondered how such a fragile bond could hold such powerful beasts. The keeper told me that when the elephants were being trained, they would first be tethered by a chain that was fastened to an iron post driven deep into the ground. The chain was fixed to a spiked collar, which fitted around the animal's ankle. Whenever an elephant pulled against the chain the spikes would pierce his leg, and he would at once yield. The trainers startled the elephants deliberately, again and again, until eventually it didn't matter how much noise was made, the elephants would always stop moving before they reached the limit of the chain. [54] From that time they could be held by a mere thread. Yet in the mind of each elephant, the cord was an invincible bond.

Isn't that a parable of us? How easily we persuade ourselves, or allow the enemy to persuade us, that our sin is unbreakable, our bondage is unchangeable! What strength we give to the cords the enemy tries to wrap around us!

Isaiah was telling those captive Israelites that their enemy was only as strong as they supposed him to be. Likewise, your foe and mine has only as much power as we give him. Rather, we should turn around and put on the strength of our God. Those who do so will no longer say, *"I am weak,"* but, *"I am strong."* They will never again lament, *"My enemy is mighty,"* but will sing, *"I am more than a conqueror through Christ who loved me and gave himself for me."* They will scorn to whisper, *"I must*

---

(54) This was not as cruel as it sounds. Since the animals were held only by a cord, if they faced any real peril they were able to break away easily, and so save their lives.

accept defeat and failure," but instead will shout, *"Blessed be God who always causes me to triumph in all things in Christ!"* Reality lies where Jesus Christ himself is. So *"put on strength and shake off those chains."*

SIT ON YOUR THRONE

What cruel ridicule there seems to be in these words, *"Rise up O captive daughter of Zion, and sit enthroned, O Jerusalem."* How could the prophet speak like that to a huddled group of terrified slaves. They were lying flat on their faces in the dust before the mighty king who has conquered them. How can they possibly stand up even, let alone ascend the throne?

Yet the prophet first looked at that trembling group of driven, frightened people; then he looked at the glittering king sitting upon his throne; yet still he demanded, *"Rise up, O captive daughter of Zion and sit yourself upon the throne!"*

The chained prisoners surely thought that Isaiah was a more bitter enemy to them than even the tyrant king. To people who surely deserved tears of compassion, a sigh of pity, a word of caring concern, Isaiah's oracle must have seemed an awful taunt, a terrible scorn, a hateful cruelty. In their helpless servitude, naked, beaten, how could they possibly clothe themselves in royal robes and take a monarch's seat?

So we are compelled to ask: what is the prophet demanding here? What is he hoping to achieve by such seeming harshness?

Simply this: *he is saying that something has to happen in the spiritual dimension before it can happen in the natural.* You and I have to change our *internal* image of ourselves before our *external* reality can be changed. We could formulate it into a law: *nothing can happen in the <u>natural</u> until it first happens in the <u>spiritual</u>.*

So this is what Isaiah was really saying –

> *As long as your image of yourself is that of a slave, as long as you believe the lies your conqueror tells about you, as long as you forget that your God has called you into a royal priesthood before his throne, you will stay in bondage. But, captive daughter of Jerusalem, you poor slaves, if only you would see yourself in a different*

image! If you would change your inner spiritual vision, then it would not be long before the world round about you would change to match it.

He said they had to do two things –

- they had to ***clothe themselves with their beautiful garments*** (vs. 1); and

- they had to ***rise up and take the throne*** (vs. 2).

Those are two very vital spiritual principles, to which we must conform ourselves: ***clothe yourself with the right garment***; and ***position yourself in the right place***.

For a monarch, those two are the essentials. No sovereign has ever reigned without both putting on the right garments and sitting in the right place.

My wife and I, on one of our trips to London, were able to watch on television the opening of the British parliament at Westminster. As you can imagine, the ceremony was conducted with much pomp and splendour, and everybody was gorgeously robed, but none more magnificently than the Queen. She came into the House splendidly arrayed and sat down on the throne, which of course is reserved for her alone. And, being *properly robed* and sitting in the *right place*, she made the pronouncements that only the ruling monarch had the authority to make. Parliament was opened, and the business of the kingdom began.

But let us imagine a different scene. We are expecting to see a king driving up to the Houses of Parliament in the royal coach, driven by elegant horses and surrounded by the royal guards – along with all the other pomp and ritual for which the British are renowned. But instead the fellow wobbles past alone on a rusty bicycle, dressed in rags. Stunned, we watch him try to enter the building and to open parliament from some small antechamber. He ignores all protocol, mumbles a few incoherent words, declares the task done, and wanders off again down the street! Everything is in chaos! Parliament cannot begin its deliberations. If the king cannot be persuaded to do the job properly, then he will have to abdicate and another take his place, someone who will dress properly, ascend the throne correctly, and speak with royal authority.

As ludicrous as that scene is, you and I have probably lived it out countless times! And then we wonder why everything goes wrong, why we have no dominion, why the enemy runs rough-shod over us! The fact is, any monarch who behaves like our fictitious king – wrongly clothed, in the wrong place, and speaking the wrong words – must forfeit all royal authority, privileges, position, and dominion. And that is what countless Christians have often done!

God has given us a royal identity in Christ, and we do not have the privilege of denying it. God has given us a royal robe to wear and a royal position in which to stand, and we cannot lawfully abrogate those gifts. We are his royal sons and daughters, and if we refuse to wear our robe or to accept the throne, then the dire consequences must fall upon ourselves, and God will accept no blame for our sorrows.

Note it again: if a monarch refuses to accept the garments given him to wear in royal majesty, and if he declines to sit upon the throne that belongs to him and to him alone, then he disgraces himself. He throws the kingdom into confusion and fools will reign where the wise should. We may see that sad scene in the kingdom of God again and again.

What is this robe, this beautiful robe, and this noble position?

1) ***The Robe*** is the righteousness that our God gives us to wear in Christ.

This "robe" teaches us to stand, not in our personal worth or our own merit, but solely, only, and always in the righteousness of Jesus himself. We should be found at all times clothed with his grace, depending on his mercy alone, trusting nothing in ourselves, and claiming nothing save what is God's own gift to us in Christ.

2) ***The Position*** is that place our God has given us in the heavenlies in Christ. For scripture tells us that the Lord has raised us up with Christ and has seated us, or enthroned us, with Christ in heavenly places. But it is not enough for this promise simply to stand in the Bible. You and I have to accept its truth and activate it by faith.

But you say, "I am lying naked and in chains in front of the Despot who has enslaved me."

That's what Israel could have said. But the prophet did not change his word. He still demanded, "O captive daughter of Jerusalem, prostrate in your bonds, clothe yourself with your beautiful robe and rise up and seize the throne!"

But they can't do that. They are naked slaves lying in chains! How can they put on a beautiful robe? How can they take a throne?

They can do it in the spirit; they can do it by faith.

And we can too. In the spirit, by faith, we can clothe ourselves with the righteousness of Jesus; we can rise up and sit upon the throne, and say, "I am reigning with Christ, I am more than a conqueror. I will not fix on the nakedness of my soul, nor on the chains that bind me. I know my God has clothed me in the heavenlies with a beautiful garment and I am sitting on the throne with him." And if we do that in the Spirit, and hold to it and refuse to let go of it, it will not be too long before it begins to occur in the natural. What is wrought in the spiritual sooner or later will be wrought in the natural.

So, to all who find yourselves in some kind of captivity – whether a captivity of soul through sin, or a captivity of the body through sickness, or a captivity of finances and lack of prosperity – to all who have been crying out to God to wake himself up and do something, this exhortation comes. You must yourself awake in the Spirit! Begin now to awaken to the promise, the presence, the opportunity of God that is at your hand. Put on your strength, the strength that is yours in the mighty arm of God. Put on your beautiful garment of righteousness, God's free gift to you in Christ. Shake off the dust of unbelief, the dust of hopeless despair. Loose your neck from those illusionary chains that the enemy has put on you, bonds that seem so strong, but are nothing more than string. And rise up and sit down on your glorious throne, positioned with Christ in righteousness and in unassailable and indestructible spiritual authority.

That is God's gift to everyone who truly believes his promise.

CHAPTER FOURTEEN:

NOT ONE SICK PERSON

Text: "God brought Israel out of Egypt, rich with silver and gold, and among all their tribes not one person was sick or feeble" (Ps 105:37).

INTRODUCTION

The number of people who marched out of Egypt may have been as many as two million! (Ex 12:37-38). Imagine a community of that size (equal to the population of San Diego, or twice the population of Adelaide) completely free from all disease, poverty, or weakness! Even allowing for some degree of poetic hyperbole, we are still presented with an extraordinary degree of divine intervention.

Was this an arbitrary, unrepeatable miracle? Can such wonders still happen?

There is no reason to suppose that supernatural succour on the same scale is not available now. Why then do we so seldom see it?

The answer may be found in the basis upon which Israel gained this miracle of divine health and strength –

THEY TRUSTED THE ATONEMENT

POWER IN THE BLOOD?

This miracle happened, we are told, as the people ate the Passover lamb (Ex 12:5-8,21-22). Disease melted away. Feebleness became strength. Weakness turned into vigour. But can the blood of a *lamb* be more effective than the Blood of the *Lamb*? Should we, dare we, expect the blood of Jesus to have less power than that of a brute beast? If the unwilling death of a finite creature could have such force, how much more energy must flow out of the voluntary sacrifice of the infinite Son of God?

But what do we mean when we talk about *"the blood"*? If Christians are not experiencing the full potential of Calvary, perhaps the reason lies in a misunderstanding what the Bible teaches about the blood of Christ.

Think about the popular hymn *There is Power In The Blood*. No doubt it has a lively melody and joyful words, but you should note that its main idea does not occur in scripture! Nowhere in the Bible is any particular energy or strength ascribed solely to the blood of the Saviour. His blood was, after all, simply ordinary human blood (albeit unstained by sin). If in those days you could have performed a laboratory analysis upon the blood of Jesus of Nazareth, you would have found nothing unusual. It had the same constituents as the blood of any healthy man, except that an analyst might have remarked that the blood of Jesus was singularly free of any taint of disease. Otherwise, it was the usual mix of natural elements.

How then does the blood work? What significance does it have?

1) ***See Exodus 12:13,23***

Note that the sprinkled blood itself did not drive away the Angel of Death, rather, the dark Spirit was deterred from striking any home that was sprinkled with blood, by the *hand of God*. That is why this event was called the *Passover*. Not because the <u>Angel</u> *"passed by"* the sprinkled homes, but because <u>God</u> *"passed over"* them (that is, overshadowed them by his own presence). Thus the Lord himself prevented the Angel of Death from attacking any of the protected homes.

The Israelites did not expect the blood of a lamb to protect them. But after the blood had been sprinkled, they did expect <u>God</u> to see it, and then to cover them himself, and so save them from the Avenger.

2)   Indeed, from that time on they always expected that whenever God saw the sprinkled blood he would respond to it in two ways –

  a) by ***protecting*** them from Satanic power

  • the Lord himself would be like a roof over their heads and a wall around them, to prevent the enemy from doing them any lasting harm (cp. Is 4:5-6); and by

  b) by ***prospering*** them in every way

  • physically, financially, spiritually (cp. 1 Th 5:23-24; 3 Jn 2).

3)   We too must see that the Blood of the Cross merely gives God a legal and righteous basis upon which to forgive us and to treat us as though we had never sinned. Indeed, it goes beyond scripture to present the *actual* blood of Christ as a weapon we can personally use in our spiritual warfare. The blood of Christ is not a kind of lucky charm, able by itself to ward off evil; it has no separate existence, nor any innate power. The blood cannot by itself deliver anyone; it does no more than provide an indestructible sanction for the **Father** to stretch out his hand and bring forgiveness and healing to those who place their trust in Christ.

Trying to impart some kind of kind of capacity for action to the blood, as if it has a conscious power to protect and prosper those who believe, tends to reduce the atonement to the level of superstition. We should scorn such pagan distortions of the gospel. Yet some teachers show a great fondness for expressions like

> *plead the blood against the devil*
> *draw a blood line*
> *nothing can cross the blood line*
> *stretch out your hands and sprinkle the blood*
> *put your mind under the blood*
> *cover yourself with the blood*
> – and so on. [55]

On the face of it, those expressions might seem harmless enough – but that depends on how they are used

- if they are used figuratively to imply no more than an appropriation by faith of the benefits of the atonement, then they may be helpful

- but if they are used to mean a literal and factual contact with the actual blood Christ spilled twenty centuries ago, then they are plainly misleading.

What then should we say about the widespread practice of

---

(55) For more on this subject see *Chapter Three* of <u>Great Words of the Gospel</u>.

PLEADING THE BLOOD?

The idea that one can go about *"pleading the blood"* contains a grave danger. When people have drawn around themselves the so-called *blood-line* [56] they tend to sit back, relax, and imagine within themselves, *"Nothing can get past the blood!"*

But that is a false security. The blood does not challenge or oppose *Satan* (as some have supposed). It does not speak to the *devil*, but to **God** (He 12:24). Satan has no fear of the ordinary human blood that flowed from Jesus' body at Calvary. Along with the blood of the criminals who were crucified with him, the blood of Jesus simply mingled with the dust, decayed, and perished. [57] *But the devil does fear the Saviour whose blood it was, and whose death, which his shed blood confirmed, has secured our redemption!*

So we must present the blood of Christ by faith, not to the *devil*, but to the *Father*, simply as a symbol of Jesus' death – as Paul said, our salvation depends only upon our sure belief that the Father raised Jesus from the dead (Ro 10:9).

So remember that the blood, by itself, has no strength to drive off Satan

- it never has been able to do anything more than provide the ground upon which we stand in the righteousness of Christ

- this then enables God to stretch out his own hand to bring us deliverance.

---

(56) How such an intangible, invisible, and mystical feat can actually be performed, baffles me!

(57) Imagine Jesus falling down and skinning his knees when he was a boy (and if he did not do so, then his humanity was not real, and we have lost our redemption). When he grazed or cut himself, he bled, just like his village friends. What happened to his blood? The same thing that happened to theirs – it trickled to the ground (or was washed away by his mother), and turned back into dust. The blood of Jesus had no magical qualities. It was just ordinary human blood.

God cannot help us while we are still reckoned sinners, but after we are pronounced righteous in Christ, then the Father may justly do for us all that lies in his heart and in his promise.

The blood of Christ is therefore not a weapon, whether of *attack* or *defence*. It is simply the evidence of Jesus' death, which becomes the basis of our justification, the ground upon which we stand when we approach God. The blood cannot offer us any protection, but *God* can and will, *because of the blood* – that is, because of what Jesus wrought at Calvary.

Likewise, the blood (the death of Christ) cannot by itself give us victory, but it does enable God to impute to us the righteousness of Christ (Ro 4:22-25). That righteousness then becomes the basis upon which we gain free access to the invincible spiritual weapons that have been given to us in Christ, and by the Word and the Spirit.

What are those weapons? They are three –

- the powerful *name* of Jesus (Mk 16:17-18)
- the mighty *promises* of God (2 Pe 1:4); and
- the supernatural *gifts* of the indwelling Spirit (Ac 1:8; 1 Co 14:7-10).

Those weapons are more than sufficient to meet every need we may have, and they are mighty to pull down every stronghold of Satan (2 Co 10:4). But they are available to, and can be used by, only those who have been reconciled to God and who have found peace through the blood of the cross (Cl 1:20).

But for the blood to be truly efficacious, two things are necessary:

ABANDONMENT TO GRACE

Notice that the Israelites and the Egyptians were a *"mixed multitude"*, displaying many different states of goodness and badness; but they did have one thing in common: *they were all under the blood!*

When God went through the land, he was not looking for Israelites, nor for Egyptians, nor even for virtuous families. His eye was searching for one thing only: *the blood!* Every family that obeyed his command and sprinkled the blood of the lamb upon its home, was protected by God from the Angel of Death, and was brought out of Egypt healthy and prosperous! No other claim was necessary, no different plea would have been accepted, no further merit could be offered. So long as God saw the blood, the family was safe. If he did not see the blood, *nothing* could protect that family from the Angel of Death.

So too, *we* must utterly forsake any hope of gaining the Father's favour by some worthy work of ours. If we are ever to approach the throne of God, it must be by the blood of Christ alone (He 10:19-22). To the merits of Christ and the sufficient work of Calvary we can add absolutely no virtue. To his grace alone we must fully abandon ourselves. We should neither want, nor dare to offer, any other plea. If God should turn away from what Jesus has done for us, then no sin-darkened work of ours will ever turn him back again. If God is content to accept us in Christ, then nothing we can do will make him more kindly disposed toward us.

> Not the labours of my hands
> Can fulfil Thy law's demands;
> These for sin could not atone;
> Thou must save, and Thou alone:
> In my hand no price I bring,
> Simply to Thy cross I cling.
> – A. M. Toplady

BOLDNESS OF FAITH

Trust in the sole efficacy of the blood to provide full and free access to the throne of God must be matched by an active expectation of divine intervention. Remember our text again: *"God brought Israel out of Egypt, rich with silver and gold, and among all their tribes not one person was sick or feeble."* The sprinkled blood of a lamb not only brought pardon to a sinful people, but also an astonishing miracle of divine deliverance.

We too, who believe in Jesus, should stir our faith into a bold assurance that God will act on our behalf, as he did on theirs, and will bring us into his Promised Land replete with *"riches and strength"*!

THEY CLAIMED THE ANOINTING

THE YOKE AND THE BURDEN

If people misunderstand the blood, even more they misunderstand the *anointing*! Thus we constantly encounter such false notions as –

> *an "anointing" is known by certain sensations or feelings*
> *you must pray until you get the "anointing"*
> *no great miracle can happen until the "anointing" falls upon you*

All those notions, and others like them, are built upon the saying, *"The anointing breaks the yoke"* – which is another phrase that does not occur in scripture! Rather, it is a corruption of *Isaiah 10:27, "The yoke shall be broken off your neck, because you carry the anointing."* What does that mean?

In his vision, Isaiah saw that Israel had fallen back into slavery, and the nation was groaning under the tyranny of Assyria. But he realised (as we saw earlier) that the people needed only to awaken to their true identity, to rediscover themselves as *"the anointed"* of God, and then the Lord would surely break off the despot's yoke. They would be freed, not *by* the anointing, but *because* they were anointed. In other words, they were *already* anointed by God, they were *already* his chosen people (which is the basic meaning of *"anointed"*); so they were *already* entitled to have every yoke loosed from off their shoulders. But nothing could happen until they came back to their *"anointing"* and on the strength of it claimed the promise of God.

In fact, they did this, and, as Isaiah had predicted, the Assyrians were driven away (see Is 36 & 37), an event that is wonderfully commemorated in Lord Byron's poetic masterpiece –

> The Assyrian came down like the wolf on the fold,
> And his cohorts were gleaming in purple and gold;
> And the sheen of their spears was like stars on the sea,
> When the blue wave rolls nightly on deep Galilee.
>
> Like the leaves of the forest when Summer is green,
> That host with their banners at sunset were seen:
> Like the leaves of the forest when Autumn hath blown,
> That host on the morrow lay withered and strown.

> For the Angel of Death spread his wings on the blast,
> And breathed in the face of the foe as he passed;
> And the eyes of the sleepers waxed deadly and chill,
> And their hearts but once heaved, and for ever grew still!
>
> . . . .
>
> And the widows of Ashur are loud in their wail,
> And the idols are broke in the temple of Baal;
> And the might of the Gentile, unsmote by the sword,
> Hath melted like snow in the glance of the Lord! [58]

Here then is the spiritual principle that is at work: God breaks off the enemy's yoke from any of his people who know the anointing!

Yet so many talk as if they had the anointing last week, lost it this week, but hope it will return next week! Have they never read the scriptures –

> *You have received an anointing from God that remains in you . . . and that anointing is real, there is nothing false about it. . . . God will never change his mind about the gifts and the calling he has given you! (1 Jn 2:27; Ro 11:27, paraphrased.)*

So it is not the *anointing* that brings deliverance. Rather, because the Lord has chosen us and called us his own, it is *God himself who* tears away every yoke. But he does so in response to faith. Freedom belongs to those who recognise that they *are* God's anointed and so refuse to be held any longer in bondage! (cp. Ga 5:1)

THE ANOINTING AND THE FAT

Two other ways to translate the text are

- *"the yoke will be broken because you have grown so fat!"*
- *"the yoke will be broken because of the oil that is upon you!"*

---

(58) The Destruction of Sennacherib, st. 1,2,3.

BECAUSE OF THE OIL

The figure is one of being consecrated to God; in the same way in which kings, priests, and others, were consecrated by having oil poured upon them.

The idea is, because Israel was an anointed (that is, consecrated) nation, God promises to deliver them.

The same idea is applicable today –

- the "anointing" does not consist of feelings, shivers, visions, nor any other kind of sensation or experience; rather it is a matter of dedication to the service of God

- if you want deliverance, then belong to God, for if you are the *"anointed"* of the Lord, then you may be confident that he will break every yoke!

See again *Isaiah 37:22*, and notice how the sinful nation, by God's grace and pardoning mercy, is now called his *"Virgin Daughter"*.

And what can she do? In her new God-given identity, she can shake off the oppressor's yoke; she can derisively *"toss her head"* as he flees in terror; she can despise and mock the one who had once held her in chains; she can assert the triumph of her God, and begin anew to rejoice in the liberty and prosperity of the Lord!

BECAUSE OF THE FAT

The figure here is that of a bullock waxing so fat and strong that it cannot be yoked (cp. De 32:15). That is, if only the people would turn back to the Lord, and renew their covenant vows to him, and once again take hold of his promise, then they would become like an enraged and full-grown bullock, too fierce and too strong to hold!

Likewise, we too should let our souls wax fat by

1) Living in the fulness of the Word

- especially by knowing who we are in Christ, which means understanding the biblical revelation of our

a) Election

Like David, when Samuel poured oil over his head, we should recognise that the first step in living as the anointed of the Lord is to know and affirm our *election* and our *calling* in Christ (1 Th 1:4; 2 Pe 1:10). Every believer is a chosen member of the most exalted company in the universe, heaven's *"royal priesthood"* (1 Pe 2:4,9-10). There is no higher or better "anointing"!

b) Consecration

We can see a picture of what "consecration" means in the anointing of the high priest of Israel. The oil that flowed over him signified his total dedication to the service of God (Le 8:12). Aaron had qualified himself to receive the sacred oil because he had already accepted the calling of God and had devoted both himself and his sons, throughout all their generations, to minister before the Lord. So long as this consecration was maintained, so long would the anointing abide.

Nor did this anointing depend upon the character of the priest. He gained his priestly office (just as we do) by right of *birth* (not by personal effort), and by sustaining his commitment to the Lord.

Unless you have wilfully renounced your divine rights, or stubbornly refuse to exercise them, then you too may be confident that *"the anointing you have received from him remains in you"*.

2) Living in the fulness of the Spirit

- which implies three things –

a) Communion

- see *Psalm 133:1-2*, which suggests that true fellowship and harmony among the people of God is like the anointing of the Lord.

b) Conviction

- when we have entered into a believing relationship with the entire Godhead; when we have an equal knowledge of the work of the Father and of the Son and of the Holy Spirit; when we know the love of God, the grace of Christ, and the comfort of the Spirit; when we are established and immovable and settled in faith, then we are indeed the anointed of the Lord (2 Co 1:19-22).

c) Completion

- that is, each believer needs to complete the stages of salvation by Holy Spirit baptism, and then to live in the quickening, revelation, and empowerment of the Spirit (1 Jn 2:20,27; 4:13; Ac 1:8; 10:38).

CONCLUSION

Those who wholeheartedly embrace these things may reckon themselves to be the Lord's anointed!

For such people the Lord will break the yoke. Then no Philistine tyranny will be able to crush them, nor will any Egyptian bondage be able to enslave them! The promise will become as true for them as it was for Israel of old –

"God brought the people out of Egypt, rich with silver and gold, and among all their tribes not one person was sick or feeble" (Ps 105:37).

BIBLIOGRAPHY

Angelology; by Ken Chant; Vision Publishing; Ramona, California.

Ante-Nicene Fathers; The; *Vol. Eight*; edited by Robert and Donaldson; 1979 reprint of the 1885 original; Eerdman's Publishing Co.; Grand Rapids, USA.

Bible Commentary of the Old and New Testaments; by Robert Jamieson, A. R. Fausset, and David Brown, 1871.

Bird's-eye View of the Bible; *Vol. 1*; Marshall, Morgan, & Scott Ltd., London, 1957.

Christianity Today Magazine; October 1987.

Dake Annotated Reference Bible, The; Dake Pub. Co. Inc., Lawrenceville, Georgia, 1963.

Demonology; by Ken Chant; Vision Publishing; Ramona, California.

Explore The Book; by J. Sidlow Baxter; *Vol. 3*; Marshall, Morgan & Scott; London, 1952.

Great Words of the Gospel; by Ken Chant; Vision Publishing; Ramona, California.

Ivanhoe; by Sir Walter Scott; Heritage Press; Norwalk, Connecticut, 1950.

Ecclesiastical History; by Eusebius; *The Martyrs of Palestine.*

New Bible Commentary; edited by G. J.Wendham, J. A. Motyer, D. A. Carson and R. T. France, 1994.

Sirach; The Apocrypha.

Week on the Concord and Merrimack Rivers, A; by Henry David Thoreau; Heritage Press; Norwalk, Connecticut, 1975.

What Luther Says; compiled by Ewald M. Plass; Concordia Publishing House; St. Louis, 1959.

Worlds In Collision; by Immanuel Velikovsky; Victor Gollancz Ltd., London, 1952.

Hymns and Poems.

A.M. Toplady; Hymn; *Rock of Ages.*

Byron; Poem; *The Destruction of Sennacherib*

Emily Dickenson; Poems; *Second Series,* 1891.
John Milton (1608-74) Poem; *Paradise Lost.*

Other Books By Ken & Alison Chant

Angelology
A study of the splendours of the heavenly realm

Attributes of Splendour
Reflections on the nature, being, and glory of God

Authenticity and Authority of the Bible
The Authenticity and Authority of scripture

Better than Revival
A Pragmatic look at Christian Ministry and the Idea of Revival

Building the Church God Wants
Not goal-setting, nor statistics, but faithfulness

Cameos of Christ
OT prophecies fulfilled in the life of Jesus

Christian Life
A positive and creative approach to life.

Clothed with Power
A Pentecostal Theology of Holy Spirit baptism.

Corinthians
Studies in 1 Corinthians

Dazzling Secrets
For Despondent Saints the causes and the cure of depression.

Demonology
Understanding and overcoming our dark enemy

Discovery
Learning and living the will of God

Dynamic Christian Foundations
Studies in Foundational Christian Truths

Emmanuel 1
Jesus: Son of Man.

Emmanuel 2
Jesus: Man who is God.

Equipped To Serve
Understanding, receiving, & using the charismata to Serve

Faith Dynamics
The limitless power of faith in God

Great Words of the Gospel
The major themes of salvation and holiness.

Healing in the New Testament
The healing covenant now.

Healing in the Old Testament
The healing covenant then.

Highly Exalted
The ascension and heavenly ministry of Christ

Mountain Movers
Secrets of mountain-moving prayer

Royal Priesthood
The priesthood of all believers.

Songs to Live By
Studies in the Psalms and Christian worship.

Strong Reasons
The Bible & Science, and the Proofs of God.

The Cross and the Crown
The passion and resurrection of Christ.

The Pentecostal Pulpit
The art of preaching in the power of the Holy Spirit.

The World's Greatest Story
The dramatic first millennium of church history

Throne Rights
Our position and spiritual authority in Christ.

Understanding Your Bible
Studies in biblical hermeneutics.

Unsung Heroines
Sage counsel for women in leadership in the church.

Walking in the Spirit
The Apostle Paul's key to successful Christian living.

When the Trumpet Sounds
Studies in the Return of Christ.

www.ingramcontent.com/pod-product-compliance
Lightning Source LLC
Chambersburg PA
CBHW060742100426
42813CB00027B/3019